THE HIDDEN
POWER
of WATCHING
and PRAYING

BOOKS BY MAHESH AND BONNIE CHAVDA

The Hidden Power of Speaking in Tongues

The Hidden Power of the Blood of Jesus

The Hidden Power of Healing Prayer

The Hidden Power of a Woman

The Hidden Power of Prayer and Fasting

The Hidden Power of Watching and Praying

40 Days of Prayer and Fasting

AVAILABLE FROM DESTINY IMAGE PUBLISHERS

THE HIDDEN
POWER

of WATCHING
and PRAYING

MAHESH AND BONNIE CHAVDA

DESTINY IMAGE® PUBLISHERS, INC.
P.O. Box 310, Shippensburg, PA 17257-0310

"Speaking to the Purposes of God for this Generation and for the Generations to Come."

This book and all other Destiny Image, Revival Press, Mercy Place, Fresh Bread, Destiny Image Fiction, and Treasure House books are available at Christian bookstores and distributors worldwide.

For a U.S. bookstore nearest you, call 1-800-722-6774.
For more information on foreign distributors, call 717-532-3040.
Or reach us on the Internet: www.destinyimage.com

ISBN 10: 0-7684-2747-9   ISBN 13: 978-0-7684-2747-9

For Worldwide Distribution, Printed in the U.S.A.
1 2 3 4 5 6 7 8 9 10 11 / 13 12 11 10 09

DEDICATION

On the eve of the Normandy invasion, 760 paratroopers from the 3rd Battalion of the 506th Parachute Infantry prepared to board planes and be dropped behind enemy lines. They and thousands of other champions would soon launch one of the most strategic assaults of World War II. Anticipation and solemn courage settled over the orchard where the paratroopers stood. Lieutenant Colonel Wolverton asked them to kneel with him in prayer:

"Do not bow your heads," Lt. Col. Wolverton said, "but look up so you can see God and ask His blessing in what we're about to do."

Those paratroopers and the countless heroes like them turned the tide of the war. The paratroopers' posture, face up in expectation as they prayed, is the spiritual posture of the watchman awake in prayer. This book is dedicated to the company of champions who have been watching and praying together since The Watch of the Lord™ began. We invite you to join with us and discover *The Hidden Power of Watching and Praying.*

THE MODEL PRAYER

Our Father in heaven,
Reveal who You are.
Set the world right;
Do what's best—as above, so below.

Keep us alive with three square meals.
Keep us forgiven with You and forgiving others.
Keep us safe from ourselves and the Devil.
You're in charge!
You can do anything You want!
You're ablaze in beauty!
Yes. Yes. Yes.

(Matthew 6:9-13 TM)

CONTENTS

INTRODUCTION

During the week of our daughter Anna's college final exams, late one evening I (Mahesh) was in my study when an urge to pray came over me strongly. Not fully understanding what this burden of prayer was about, I began to pray in the Spirit.[1]

For nearly three hours, I remained in this state of prayer, at one point kneeling beside the couch where I had been sitting. Eventually the urge to pray lifted as it had come. As I went off to bed, I passed by the room where Anna was still up studying. Poking my head in the door, having given no specific thought to what I was about to say, I told her, "Instead of taking my car to school tomorrow as you usually do, take your mother's Jeep." Momentarily interrupted, Anna looked up from her books and nodded.

I repeated this command twice more, until Anna rolled her eyes and said, "OK Dad, I promise."

The next morning, our house phone began to ring just before 8 o'clock. When Bonnie answered the phone, the caller informed us that Anna had been involved in a terrible car accident just beyond our neighborhood. We rushed to the scene of the crash.

When we got there, the air was still filled with a white cloud from the air bags, which had deployed. At the scene, patrolmen, two fire engine details, and an EMS unit were working. The front of Bonnie's Jeep was wrapped around a tree in a shallow ravine just beyond a hairpin turn in the road. An early rain had left the road surfaces slippery and, blinded by the morning sun, Anna had lost control of the vehicle. Skidding off the road, she had hit the tree head-on at approximately 35 miles per hour. The vehicle was totaled and Anna was pinned inside.

As the EMS team worked to extract our daughter from the vehicle, all involved were certain that our daughter was surely dead or dying. Bonnie ran to the open door just as the emergency team lifted Anna out. She was alive, although both of her legs were broken. The officials on the scene kept repeating, "It's a miracle. It's a miracle your daughter is alive." A career patrolman and experienced fire rescue and EMS personnel all told us this was the first of such accidents they had ever seen where the person in the car was not instantly killed. "Those airbags," they said. "The airbags saved her."

The first miracle in this testimony is the miracle of being awakened to prayer. The urge to pray that came on me the night before the accident was a prophetic breath from our Father in Heaven, who neither slumbers nor sleeps. He was watching over Anna. As I prayed in the Spirit, I had been breathing out the will of the Father to save Anna's life during the events that were to occur the next morning.

The second miracle was the instruction that I gave to Anna, which came as a result of my long prayer, the insistent instruction to take her mother's car instead of mine as she usually did. (My vehicle did not have airbags.)

The third and greatest miracle was the result of the first two. Our daughter is alive and well today.

This is a story of watching in prayer. The thief who comes to steal, kill, and destroy must pass by the house where watch lamps are brightly burning. One alert watchman can save an entire house. This is why Paul wrote to the Thessalonian church, *"pray without ceasing"* (1 Thess. 5:17).

In the life of Jesus, we can see an example of how a person becomes prayer and is able to "pray without ceasing." Going about His daily routine, Jesus suddenly began to pray:

> *Abruptly Jesus broke into prayer: "Thank You, Father, Lord of heaven and earth. You've concealed Your ways from sophisticates and know-it-alls, but spelled them out clearly to ordinary people. Yes, Father, that's the way You like to work"* (Matthew 11:25-26 TM).

Jesus was a watchman. He drew His closest friends into that circle of prayer. They drew in many more, as believers were added to the Church. That praying Church turned the world's culture on its ear.

We have been privileged to live a life watching in prayer. Watching in prayer is the nuclear weapon of the Church in any age, particularly if two or more are gathered in His name. We have seen the hidden power of watching in prayer to bring the Kingdom of God on earth thousands of times over in deliverances, in healings, in reconciliation, in restoration of individuals, families, churches, nations.

The earliest prayer posture of Christianity—face-up in expectation—reflects the attitude of an awakened spirit. Prayer "without ceasing" is not limited to prayer on one's knees or even to prayer with eyes closed reverentially. In fact, "watching in prayer" implies open eyes and an alert spirit. It can happen wherever a believer finds himself or herself, and it is particularly powerful when the person is not isolated from others.

The model prayer of Jesus, traditionally called the "Our Father" or "The Lord's Prayer," is a perfect summary of the most important aspects of watchful prayer. Far more than a few rote phrases to be repeated in a singsong religious fashion, this simple prayer of Jesus is the spinal column of all spiritual revelation, foundational to the prayers of every believer.

The men who went about with Jesus did not always fully grasp what they observed in His life. Jesus' prayer life was revolutionary. Christ's disciples had come from a 3000-year-old tradition of prayer and Jesus did too. Yet there was something different about the way Jesus prayed. When they saw it, His friends said, "Teach us to pray the way You do!" So He gave them the model prayer.

One of history's most powerful prayer warriors, Teresa of Avila, proposed that praying the "Our Father" with revelation knowledge and personal experience of God would be sufficient to raise a Christian to the heights of prayer intended by God.[2] It is with this in mind we have written this book with our prayers that you will become an effective watchman for your world, bringing down Heaven to earth through your prayers.

What was different about Jesus' prayers? His prayer began in Heaven with His Father. Jesus Christ became our intercessor before intervention was necessary! He lives on, interceding for you and me today (see Romans 8:34). He is always joined with the Father.

The One who neither slumbers nor sleeps is always looking for men and women who count sheep and are willing to watch over His flocks by day and night. At the beginning of time, God intervened and said, "Let there be light!" At the end of time, Christ shall intervene when He comes to set the world right. In between these two events, there hangs a great suspension bridge over which the watchmen of God walk with Him in prayer. This bridge connects Heaven and earth. Believers who are awake to watch and pray pass between the two realms, harmonizing with God in His desires for earth.

In the context of fulfilling his call as a watchman, Jeremiah speaks of the justice of God's judgment:

> *Run to and fro through the streets of Jerusalem; see now and know; and seek in her open places if you can find a man, if there is anyone who executes judgment, who seeks the truth, and I will pardon her* [Jerusalem] (Jeremiah 5:1).

Eyes wide open to the crises of his generation, the prophet also had spirit-eyes through which he discerned God's readiness to intervene if He could find someone who was awake and in harmony with His will.

As with the story of our daughter Anna, prayer begins to create the solution before the problem exists. Prayer arrives on the scene, already intervening as the problem unfolds. Prayer remains behind after the crisis is over to pick up the pieces and to recreate what has been destroyed. Prayer revitalizes the wasted land and brings forth a seed-bearing garden. By watching in prayer, light is sown in darkness, the foundations are reestablished, and the pleasure of God is fulfilled. Prayer never ceases. It continues, in season and out, anticipating, observing, plowing, sowing, reaping, fertilizing, watering, and rejoicing.

Living our lives with eyes open for God is what watching in prayer is all about. This is the striking difference in Jesus' prayer life. Prayer is being in harmony with our Father in Heaven and allowing Him to make us a vessel of His will on earth. Watching in prayer is developing a posture of militant vigilance with a spirit fully awakened to God. It is not so much doing something different as it is *being* different in prayer.

As we began to put this book on paper, we were blessed to spend a few days in retreat on the lake home of dear friends. The first morning we watched from the deck as a man took his son out into the lake to teach him to swim. After splashing about a bit, the man slid onto his back and said to the boy, "You see? It's just like lying on the couch." Although there was nothing to support his body from falling into the depths, the boy so trusted his father, almost immediately he was imitating him, swimming back and forth and happily "lying on the couch" in between. The boy did not become someone else in order to swim and float. As he watched his father, he imitated him.

Like the man on the lake, there is a way for us to rest, to float, as we watch in prayer. We learn not to succumb to the elements of chaos in our lives or to the darkness in our generation. As we learn to watch with Jesus, we learn to succumb to the rhythms of God. We learn by watching Jesus watch the Father. Jesus watched in prayer when He walked the earth, and He still watches in prayer. He wants us to join Him.

Jürgen Moltmann wrote: "Prayer never stands by itself. It is always bound up with watching,...which goes with true praying, and to which true prayer is supposed to lead us. Praying is good, but watching is better."[3]

As a soldier in Hitler's army during World War II Moltmann witnessed terrible things. He surrendered to the first British soldier that came along. During his internment as a prisoner of war, he met Christians who so impacted him that he committed his life to Christ. "What else is Christian spirituality except watching and praying, watching prayerfully and praying watchfully?" he wrote. "Strong men often think that praying is something for old women who have nothing left to them but the rosary or the hymn-book. It has become rather unknown that praying has to do with awakening, watching, attention, and the expectation of life."[4]

As Moltmann observed:

> Christian faith is not blind faith. It is the wakeful expectation of God, which touches all the senses. The early Christians prayed standing up, looking up, with arms outstretched and eyes wide open, ready to walk or to leap forward. Their prayer posture reflects tense expectation, not quiet heart searching. "We do not watch just because of the dangers that threaten us. We are expecting the salvation of the world. We are watching for God's advent. With tense attention, we open all our senses for the coming of God into our lives, into our society, to this earth."[5]

The Watchman of the Father is brooding over His nest to create a dwelling place for God. He is walking in the garden of His creation. He is praying in Gethsemane. He is looking for His friends and calling them to come. He is saying, "Collect your faculties. Rise up from sitting and lying down. Come! Be vigilant with Me!" Christ told his disciples, *"What I say to you, I say to all: Watch!"* (Mark 13:37).

We are face-up in expectation, getting ourselves and our world ready for His appearing as we discover the power of watching in prayer. And we invite you to watch with us!

ENDNOTES

1. See First Corinthians 12-14 and Mahesh Chavda, *The Hidden Power of Speaking in Tongues* (Shippensburg, PA: Destiny Image, 2003).
2. Teresa of Avila, *The Way of Perfection.*

3. Jürgen Moltmann and Elisabeth Moltmann-Wendel, *Passion for God: Theology in Two Voices* (Louisville, KY: Westminster-John Knox Press, 2003), 57.

4. Ibid.

5. Ibid., 62-63.

CHAPTER 1

Reveal Who You Are

Our Father in Heaven...

THE REVELATION OF THE FATHER, FOUNDATION FOR ALL PRAYER.

"Finis origine pendet," the Roman poet Manlius wrote. "The end depends on the beginning."

The beginning of our watching in prayer began many years ago. During the charismatic renewal of the 1970s, it became our custom to forego regular periods of sleep for the sake of prayer. Coupled with fasting at times, we joined together with friends in private homes for times of worship, prayer, and Bible teaching. This lifestyle flowed into our church life as we took up our first pastorate, and has continued in every place and in every season for more than three decades.

In 1994, we moved to Charlotte, North Carolina, and a visitation of renewal poured out in our home. We gathered a few friends to fellowship and pray together on Friday nights. The Lord said to us, "Watch with Me," and The Watch of the Lord was born.

In those days I (Mahesh) received a vision which recurred three times over three weeks. In the vision I saw huge feet in the midst of the room. When I asked the Lord, "What does it mean?" I got no answer, just big feet. The next week, I got the same vision again, except this time the feet were surrounded by clouds. The third week, the vision came, and this time I saw that the clouds around the feet were filled with golden glory, lightning, love, blessings, and power. The clouds parted for a moment, and I saw that the feet were scarred by nail prints. Immediately the Holy Spirit spoke to me: "Go to Ruth, chapter 3. My voice is the voice of Naomi." Here's what I found.

In the book of Ruth, Jewish Naomi instructs her Gentile daughter-in-law:

> *Wash and perfume yourself, and put on your best clothes. Then go down to the threshing floor, but don't let [Boaz] know you are there until he has finished eating and drinking. When he lies down, note the place where he is lying. Then go and uncover his feet and lie down. He will tell you what to do* (Ruth 3:3-4 NIV).

From this, we realized that watching is a bridal relationship. It's an intimate thing. It is like coming to "uncover the feet of the Lord" and then waiting for Him to tell us what to do. The Holy Spirit is directing us to spend the night at Jesus' feet. Just like Boaz did, as we come to watch and pray, Jesus takes us under His wing, protecting us, rejoicing that we have chosen to follow the voice of His Spirit over the other pulls and distractions of the world. We come to the threshing floor where He winnows us, purifying us to be His spotless Bride. We come to set aside our own agendas and needs to avail ourselves to His agenda and purpose in this hour. Just as Naomi told Ruth, "He will tell you what to do," as we come into His presence, we are assured that He will tell us what to do. This is the key that sets apart watching prayer from some of our previous misconceptions of intercession.

Watching is the art of being in God's presence, enjoying Him, worshiping Him, and listening for His instruction. It is in that place of being in relationship that He will instruct us. He leads by the Holy Spirit and provides insight, instruction, and direction regarding His plans and strategies in battle. When He directs, we bind the enemy, we pray for healing and deliverance and we anoint people with oil, and we find that He is willing to do all that we ask.

So we gathered a few believers and began to stay up all night, every week on Friday night, watching in prayer. We had some amazing healings of cancer and diabetes and terminal conditions right from the beginning. The presence of the Lord was so thick that people would come from across the country in buses to join us in prayer and worship.

We have kept watching in prayer for over fourteen years straight now, every Friday night. The Bridegroom of Heaven is listening to our requests, and we have seen Him intervene in national and international events, and in our personal and family lives. He has been telling us what to do as we have been keeping The Watch together.

When Ruth left in the morning, Boaz heaped her shawl full of grain. We have found that the same happens for us when we come to lie at the feet of our Kinsman-Redeemer, Jesus. As the morning light begins to break, we find that He has filled us with His blessings as we have spent the night at His feet.

BEGINNING TO WATCH

Where do we begin in our approach to watching in prayer? Jesus began teaching His disciples to pray with these words: "Our Father in Heaven."

Prayer is difficult for many because they have never appropriated the truths of God's fatherhood. The God to whom we pray is Father. Genuine Christian prayer begins with the realization that when we receive Christ we are born into the most remarkable family imaginable. We become the sons and daughters of the Father, brothers and sisters of Jesus Christ, welcomed into oneness with the Holy Spirit. Knowing God as Father is the key to Christian prayer.

This knowledge enables us to become fully human, because the essence of humanness is relationship. Relationship indicates there is a community to which we are related. (We will explore the joys and values of sharing in ongoing community of prayer in Chapter 3.)

There are as many ideas of who God is as there are world religions, but Christianity is not just another world religion. Christian faith is a living, personal relationship made real through the mystery of the working of the Holy Spirit. No other prophet, guru, potentate, angel, or visitor from an alien planet has made such a bold claim as Jesus has. The Father has taken the initiative to send His Son to become our elder brother who paves our way back home. No salvation offered by any other self-proclaimed spokesman for God is remotely similar. Mohammed claims Allah has no sons and no companions, nor has any need of them. Buddha, Krishna, Mohammed, and the hosts of other figures who have claimed to have the truth about God are all dead. None of them claimed to be a sin offering in exchange for our sins. Few of them even gave hope that some kind of salvation was possible. Those who did laid a heavy burden of religious regulations on their followers.

All of the figures down through history claiming to reveal God to man also confessed that they had failed to keep the very religions they invented. All of their "gods" stand at a distance behind a veil of obscurity, threatening or being threatened. None of them claimed that the ultimate revelation of God is as our Father who loves us on a personal and intimate level.

Only Jesus said, "I have come to give you life abundantly." Not only did Jesus completely keep the commands He gave to others, but also, after His resurrection, He showed Himself to over five hundred people. They touched His side and hands, ate the food He cooked for them, talked with Him, received His instructions for the future, saw His glory, and stood watching as He went up and disappeared into Heaven with a joyful promise of returning in like manner. He said, "I am going to the Father to prepare a place for you so that where I AM you may be, too!" (See John 14:2-3.)

In one of the earliest accounts of a man inquiring who God is, Moses asked, "Who shall I say has sent me?" God replied: "Tell them I AM that I AM has sent you."[1] Jesus asked His disciples, "Who do men say that I AM?" The men gave a variety of answers. Then He asked, "But who do *you* say that I am?" Peter said, "You are the Christ, the Son of the Living God." Jesus answered, "Blessed are you, Simon son of Jonah for flesh and blood has not revealed this to you but My Father who is in Heaven. And upon this rock I will build My church and the gates of hell will not prevail against it" (see Matt.16:13-18).

Jesus is the Son of the Father. He is the exact representation and image of the One who created your world. When Jesus takes your hand, He leads you straight to the Father. You find yourself planted on an immovable foundation of truth from which all other truth flows. No power can stand against this truth.

Human nature seems most comfortable in keeping God at a distance. People tend to fear or squirm or curse or run if He seems to get too close to home or too near the heart. God is much less threatening if He is an impersonal "higher power" rather than the One to whom we give a relational account for ourselves and our lives.

The earliest account of a name being assigned to this I AM God is in the words to a man who came to be known as the father of faith. "Do not fear, Abram, I AM your Shield, your exceedingly great reward!" (See Genesis 15:1.) A shield? The Hebrew shield or *magen* is a personal buckler used to defend one's torso during hand-to-hand combat with an enemy. *Magen* was also used as a word for "king" in a context where every city had a god-king; and every one of those god-kings was struggling to become the chief over all other kings in the territory. When Abraham came into the land that God had promised him there would be five territorial kings he would have to defeat. But God said, "Don't worry...I AM King and will give this land over to you and your sons." Abraham laid aside the name and the inheritance his earthly father would have allotted him. He chose to obey the voice of Father God. Moses, too, refused the name and inheritance due him as a son of Pharaoh, choosing the name and inheritance as a son of Abraham. Abraham and Moses believed in I AM of the Bible.

Coming Home

What if this God of the Bible is who He says? What does that mean for us? How do I relate to Him? Does He have a plan for my life? Is it a good plan? Does He have a plan for the world? Do I fit into His plan? Who is 'the God of Abraham, Isaac, and Jacob'? Who is the God who made the worlds, told Noah to build an ark, parted the Red Sea, made David sing, filled the ancient temple with the glory, spoke through the prophets, chose Israel as His own possession, and became the Man who went to Calvary? Who is I AM?

Jesus began to reveal Himself to me (Bonnie) when I was nineteen years old. At a certain point, I lay down the identity of my father's proud heritage to follow Jesus. But within weeks of a powerful renewal experience, dark shadows from the world began to torment me. I knew my natural father could not help. A friend invited me to attend a prayer meeting in a fellow Christian's home, one of the many midweek renewal meetings happening across the nation during the days of the charismatic outpouring. With the exception of the friend, I did not know any of the other people who would be attending that night.

When I walked through the door, I was overcome by an intense atmosphere of a very real God. It was as though His Person hung in molecules filling up the air. Although I could not see Him with my physical eyes, my heart embraced Him and shouted, "I'm home at last!" The perfect strangers in the room were suddenly closer than natural family members who did not know Christ.

As I encountered the pure presence of God, He adopted me. Although I had more or less grown up in church and had a "salvation moment" as a child, I had gone my own way for my teen years and had never before felt the love of my heavenly Father. Over the next few weeks I launched upon a spiritual journey in God that has become a lifetime of adventure, being baptized in the Holy Spirit and powerfully delivered. This is what it means to receive the spirit of adoption.

A Story of Return

Without intimacy with God as Father, a person may seek himself in all sorts of things. Some search for "fulfillment," craving affirmation or pleasure. Some are just looking to survive. But everyone who is searching for something is actually looking for someone—the Father who made us in His image. The prodigal son left his father and found himself the slave of a cruel master (see Luke 15). In our search for identity, the prince of this world (the devil) will send each of us "into his fields to feed swine." The best day of the lost boy's life was the day he woke up in a pigsty starving for something real. In the shadows of his searching, God was lurking—just as He still does today. He is calling us as he did to Adam: "Where are you?" No more hiding. There are great dreams to be dreamed, adventures to be lived, battles to be won and lives to be saved.

The prodigal son was no orphan but when he went away from his father, he was existing as if he were a hired hand. Many of us have already gone down this road into the far country, believing the world's systems offer us something that we want. But only if we return to our Father can we find the One who can satisfy.

Don't waste your inheritance; don't disdain the table that God has spread for you. Whether you are in the Kingdom or out of it, whether you are backslidden or fully walking with the Lord, there is more at the Father's table than you have had so far. God has made this day for you that He may reveal who He is. Like the prodigal's father, our Father is still watching and waiting.

When we find our way back, we are able to turn to help out in the Father-directed search for our missing family members. We seek them in prayer. We seek them in love. We watch with expectancy from day to day, ready to celebrate their return.

It's simple, really. To whom do you pray? There are streams of healing, of deliverance, of reconciliation and revelation, of hope, peace, contentment, security, and fearlessness that come in the revelation of God as our Father. In Christ we are no longer just servants, no longer merely acquaintances, no longer lowly slaves, no longer only ministers, no longer just ambassadors. Through the blood of Christ, we come *home*. The Great Architect has designed a luxury home for Himself by making human beings in His image. His ultimate residence is within the human heart. The human spirit is the Holy of Holies. It is God's desired resting place. The Shekinah glory that lifted from the temple in the days of Ezekiel was silent after Malachi prophesied, never appearing again until the day of Pentecost. He is returning to His dwelling place in you, in me, in us. When you are able to embrace God as your Father, the gates of hell cannot prevail against you.

Jesus refers to God more than a hundred times in the Gospels. Fewer than half a dozen of those references to God are as anything other than "Father." Jesus calls God "My heavenly Father," "My Father," "your Father," "your heavenly Father," "the Father," and "the heavenly Father." Today, allow Him to fully embrace you as your Father, and in return fully embrace Him back as a son or daughter, no longer considering yourself an unworthy hired servant.

Each of us has been made worthy of God's embrace and inheritance because of Christ the Son. On the Cross, Jesus "became sin for us." You died. I died. And then we rose up to new life again. When we say, *"God so loved the world that He gave His only begotten Son,"* it's the same as when the father said to his servants, *"Bring out the best robe and put it on him and put a ring on his hand and sandals on his feet. And bring the fatted calf here and kill it, and let us eat and be merry; for this my son was dead and is alive again; he was lost and is found"* (John 3:16 and Luke 15:22-24). In the present-day revival of prayer, the feasting has begun. Pull your chair up and eat to your heart's content from the banquet table. Taste and see how good God really is!

> *"For you did not receive the spirit of bondage again to fear, but you received the Spirit of adoption by whom we cry out, 'Abba, Father'"* (Romans 8:15).

Receiving the Spirit of Adoption

Just before I (Mahesh) turned five years old, my father died, essentially leaving me not only fatherless, but with very little living knowledge of my father.

When I was sixteen years old, all that changed. A Baptist missionary knocked on our door one day and asked for a drink of water. In return for that glass of water, she gave me a New Testament. I had been raised in a family of aristocratic Hindu tradition with a long written family history. For eight hundred years, my family had been defenders of the Hindu faith. But I was also a lover of truth.

Being an avid reader, I spent the next few nights reading this book. It was an interesting book, not like any I had ever read before. It seemed as if, while I read it, the Author was looking over my shoulder and reading me. After two or three nights of this, I began to come to a crisis in my identity, because I realized that everything this book was about was against my natural, cultural, and religious heritage. I made a decision that I wasn't going to read that book anymore.

That night, however, I suddenly fell into a trance-like sleep at my little reading table, and my consciousness was taken to a place and a realm that I had never before visited. I found myself in a place that was more real than anything I had ever experienced. The streets were of gold, the atmosphere was filled with singing, and vibrant colors and zillions of beams of light were dancing all around. The light was alive and so full of joy that my entire being was in ecstasy, filled with the atmosphere of Heaven. Every beam of light was singing to me and every beam of light had a variation of one theme: "I love you; I love you; I love you. I have always loved you; I'll always love you; I died for you before you ever knew Me, for I always loved you. I love you; I will always love you."

And then I saw the source of light coming toward me. The light was a Person. I knew immediately that it was Jesus. I looked into Jesus' eyes and saw the fire of His love. I saw eyes that had shed every tear and that knew every joy. And then the One whom

I knew loved me most in the universe came and put His hand right on my shoulder and said, "My little brother."

When I woke up, the Bible was turned to a place I had not remembered reading. It was open at the story of a rich young ruler who came to Jesus one day, asking what he could do to inherit eternal life. When Jesus gave him the answer, it says that the young man went away very sorrowful, because he was unwilling to make that exchange.

What must a man do to inherit eternal life? He must get to know the Father. How does he get to know Him? By receiving the Son. I did it. I became Jesus' newest brother, the newest adopted son of our Father, and I knew He would never die or leave me.

If your Father were the King, the president, the Supreme Court judge, the greatest defense attorney, the Olympic champion, the world-class artist, the brain surgeon, the greatest philosopher, the greatest business man, the richest man in the world—these things would be your heritage. You would have personal access to the best of every realm because the One who is your Father is also all of those things to the world. This is what you possess once you come to Christ and God becomes your Father.

We who have received Christ have received the Father. As we have His Spirit we also receive His heart and with it deliverance from the world through the very body and blood of Christ. We discern between the holy and the unholy. We rejoice in our new identity. This is not worldly wisdom. We are holding onto God Himself, and we are holding to a system of values as ancient as the Ancient of Days Himself, one that supersedes contemporary cultural fads and popular societal trends.

As we lean on God, there will also be a mutual leaning upon one another, elder generations leaning upon the faithful young for their zeal, talent, fresh insight, and support and the young leaning upon their elders for their foundational, experiential wisdom and tested knowledge of God and His ways.

Letting Him Nurture You

Once you have received the spirit of adoption and you recognize God as your Father, you will be willing to receive His correction. Correction is a blessing. We have a heavenly Father as we have earthly fathers. We have spiritual fathers as we have natural ones.

Paul compares his role as an apostle to the role filled by a father: *"For though you might have ten thousand instructors in Christ, yet you do not have many fathers; for in Christ Jesus I have begotten you through the gospel"* (1 Cor. 4:15).

We live in a somewhat dysfunctional culture, but our children prosper under the covering of the Church. There may not be natural fathers in every family but the Spirit-filled church that takes prayer and covering seriously is a great blessing. As you benefit from the covering of the Church, be thankful. The Church is the Father's house.

Jesus' mission to earth is to reveal the Father. At one point some of the men who followed Jesus said, "Show us the father and that will be sufficient." He replied, "If you have seen Me you have seen the Father." (See John 14:8-9.) If you want to see the face of God, turn the eyes of your heart on Jesus. When a person lays hold of this revelation of God as Father everything else falls in place.

This is the foundation of watching in prayer. It's where we begin our journey. Adam and Eve lost their way early when they went their own way, breaking God's command. The memory of God was soon lost, too. In every generation, more and more people grew farther and farther away from the knowledge of who God really is. Then they began to invent their own versions of God and make religions around their inventions. But God remained true.

The way home has been opened through the sacrifice made on Calvary. Jesus ploughed the road back to the Father when he took the cat-o'-nine-tails on his back. He opened the road with His blood. We pray our way home with an awakened spirit, watching in prayer with our Father. As we return to unbroken fellowship with Him, He raises us as His own sons and daughters. And so we see how Jesus was able to say, "In that day you will ask Me (Jesus) nothing, most certainly I tell you whatever you ask the Father in My name...He will do it!" (See John 16:23.)

And so we pray, "Our Father, reveal who You are."

ENDNOTE

1. See Exod. 3:13-14. (Moses at the burning bush.)

CHAPTER 2

Holy!

...*Hallowed Be Your Name*...

RESTORING HONOR.

It was nearing midnight at our regular Friday night prayer watch, and 100 prayer warriors were standing on the threshold of a breakthrough as they watched together in prayer. This spiritual battalion was made up of seasoned disciples, new converts, and watchmen-in-training. The worship leader transitioned into a song that magnified Jesus as the Lamb. The whole company began to harmonize in their spirits with the vibration of Heaven.

It was as though there were circles of increasing Presence emanating from the throne of Heaven, as if the Lord had dropped a pearl into the pool of our corporate worship and greater and greater circles of prayer and praise began to radiate from the center. Although we could not see Him with our physical eyes, the entire body of watchmen suddenly "saw" Jesus together. Our spirits opened in unison and suddenly, mysteriously, all of us were together in Heaven on earth. It's hard to describe the ecstasy of such a moment.

For a long time, the congregation was like one great tuning fork, vibrating with one heart in unity of minds and senses to the sound of Heaven and the presence of the Lamb. It was evident there were angels and other majestic hosts with us.

A chant that carried a sound of singing grew louder and louder. Those hundred voices resounded as thousands. The sound cleared the atmosphere. It became easy to think with God, feel with God, hear with God, see with God, speak with God. The shadows of burdens or failures or bondages that people had carried in with them evaporated in this holy atmosphere. Anything became possible.

The only word we heard was, "Holy!" Together, every voice began to say, "Holy, Holy, Holy!" That was the only word with which we could respond to the unutterably holy Presence. Contained within it seemed to be an echo of every other word that can describe the infinite facets of God's beauty. Without paying attention to each other, the watchmen began to prostrate themselves in the glory. For more than an hour, we resonated with Heaven, although it seemed like a few seconds because we were in pure ecstasy.

The resonance began to change and move people to rise and twirl or dance or *daven* (the Hebrew word for the form prayer that involves a rhythmic bending of the knee and bowing forward). Many of us experienced a kind of peripheral spiritual vision—there to our right, to our left—we seemed to glimpse living creatures moving back and forth among the watchmen.

Just when it seemed our hearts would burst, there was a release, a breakthrough. Without having to repeat days, weeks, months, and years of praying words for our families, all those prayers were answered. The Lamb in our midst became our

Amen—the "So Be It"—of every life in The Watch. It would have taken many hours and many pages to go to the watchmen one by one, listen to their prayer requests, say them out and agree together on them. An hour of heavenly symphony accomplished what it would have taken days to accomplish through corporate prayer.

It was as if a mighty wave washed over us and rolled back into the cosmos. Like precious shells tossed up on a seashore, words of prophecy, visions, and words of knowledge were released out of our hearts for those around us. Additionally, there was a fresh immediacy in our knowledge of the fact that the Lord of Glory reigns from His throne over our world. National concerns, international threats, economic crises, wars and rumors of wars, all were bowing under His feet. We felt history was changing that night. *"Holy, Holy, Holy is God-of-the-Angel-Armies. His bright glory fills the whole earth. The foundations trembled at the sound of the angel voices, and then the whole house filled with smoke"* (Isa. 6:3-4 TM). This must be what it means to rule and reign with Him as we watch together in prayer!

It is quite a life-changing moment when an individual is caught up in such an intimate experience of the living God, but it is quite another when it happens corporately. We believe this is the prayer that God is restoring and releasing in this hour, and it is the prayer of the watchmen.

HALLOWED—IT'S ALL HIS

When we come into the revelation of the holy, awesome splendor of our Father who loves us, it turns our hearts toward Him, His will, and His Kingdom. Just as Jesus did in His prayer, our mouths express, "Our Father, how awesome You are!" In this revelation of His holiness, our hearts and our minds and our beings resonate with all of the rest of Jesus' prayer.

When we pray, "hallowed be Your name," we pray for ourselves and our enemies according to the complete will of God. When Jesus taught us to pray "hallowed be Your name," He was gathering God's praying army on the earth. When He taught us to pray "hallowed be Your name," He was teaching us to pray for our sanctification and return. "Come out from among them and be separate. You shall be holy unto Me for I the Lord am holy" (see 2 Cor. 6:17 and 1 Pet. 1:16).

When He taught us to pray "hallowed be Your name," He was teaching us to pray also for our enemies. He was teaching us to harmonize with the predetermination of God to restore His covenant and judge His enemies who will not relent of their evil deeds. The prophet Ezekiel said,

> *You will come up against My people Israel like a cloud, to cover the land. It will be in the latter days that I will bring you against My land, so that the nations may know Me, when I am hallowed in you…before their eyes.…And it will come to pass at that same time…that my fury will show in My face* (Ezekiel 38:16,18).

God will make a show of His strength when He comes against the destroyer and all those who will not turn from their determination to destroy His people. As He confronts their rebellion, His name will be revered as holy in the sight of all who witness this great battle, and the nations will come to know Him as the One who is hallowed in that battle. All will see that He is God and that He is worthy to be worshipped and served.

"Hallowed be Your name" is a prayer for the revelation of Jesus Christ to come upon the earth. It is a prayer for harvest. It is a prayer for judgment. It is a prayer for the restoration of the glory. It is a prayer for God's manifest presence among His people. It is a prayer for holiness that adorns His house. It is a prayer for the restoration of His dwelling place on earth as it is in Heaven. It is a prayer that the Father be revealed.

Power in the Name

In one of our campaigns in Africa, a woman brought her nine-year-old daughter to receive a blessing. To come into supernatural blessing, often we must first remove any obstacles we have purposely or inadvertently established in our lives. I (Mahesh) prayed a general prayer to break any personal and family line curses, calling out sorcery and witchcraft specifically. This young girl began screaming, "Mamma! Mamma! My knee hurts! My knee hurts!" Her mother saw blood coming from her daughter's knee. Suddenly, before our very eyes, a big needle popped out of the girl's body! We have a picture of that needle.

This was not as strange as you might suppose. Her mother told us that when a baby was born, it was customary in her village to consult a sorcerer for spells of protection over a child's life. The village witchdoctor had inserted this needle into her little baby daughter, and it had stayed there for nine years. But when I had said, "In the name of Jesus, I break every curse of sorcery," the spell had been broken and its emblem came out of the girl's body.

God made us to share in His own divine nature. This is what it means to be "holy"—fully consecrated to God, His ways and His purpose. The One who does this work in us as we yield to him is called the *Holy* Spirit.

As we exchange breath for breath with Him in prayer that never ceases, that Breath of holy life fills and transform us into His own likeness, so that we can walk in the victory of the Spirit, joyfully facing opposition from the kingdoms of this world. With the empowering action flowing from pure virtue, you have an invincible army. When old and young together support one another in vision, drawing from the strength of true virtue and holding to values ordained by Heaven, victory is at hand.

These are days of revival that Malachi prophesied. The mark of God is transgenerational. These are a people who fear the Lord and call upon Him in truth: a people who walk in inner light and manifest Spirit wisdom and power when chaos and confusion abound, a people formed and trained in the nurture and admonition of God. *"The night is far spent, the day is at hand. Therefore let us cast off the works of darkness, and let us put on the armor of light"* (Rom. 13:12).

Reverence

We are entering into a new phase of Church history. It is an era that requires a fresh honor in our heart-attitudes and in our conduct toward His name. In First Samuel we read: *"Therefore the Lord God of Israel says: '...those who honor Me I will honor, and those who despise Me shall be lightly esteemed'"* (1 Sam. 2:30). Jesus gave His life for us. He has earned every honor, and so we say *"Worthy is the Lamb...to receive power and riches and wisdom, and strength and honor and glory and blessing!"* (Rev. 5:12). Worthy is the Lamb! Hallowed be Your name.

As we revere Him, we hallow Him. When we hallow Him, it affects our lives; it alters our values and our actions. When we hallow Him, that which is wrong in His sight becomes wrong in our sight. So our worship affects not just our hearts, but also our actions. Our decisions do not come from keeping a set of "do's and don't's," but rather they come from a heart of reverence for His name.

David knew the secret of "hallowed be Your name." When he saw that big giant with that big sword, he said, "Who is this uncircumcised Philistine that should defy the armies of the living God and profane the Name of the God of Israel?" (see 1 Sam. 17:26). He had jealousy for the name of God. He was saying, "Goliath, you are not just threatening us, you are profaning the name of the God of Israel, the name I revere, and that's the reason I'm going to take your head off right now." And he did.

The more you hallow the name of God in your heart, the more your Goliaths will be defeated. That doesn't make you sanctimonious, and it doesn't make you legalistic. It makes you holy as He is holy—holy and free. There is a big difference between hallowing the name and getting religious.

Abraham honored His name, and then God showed him the height and the depth of the *glory* of His name. It was as if He said, "All right, and I'm going to reveal Myself to you, because you reverenced My name. I am going to give you a living revelation. I am *Jehovah Jireh*, the Lord your Provider." Moses reverenced His name and God revealed Himself as *Jehovah Raphe*, the Lord that healeth thee. Joshua reverenced His name and God revealed Himself as *Jehovah Sabaoth*, the Captain of the armies of the Living God.

Restoration of Honor

As we recover the foundation of honor for God and for His Word, He will show us His glory.

We are listening to the Son as He listened to the Father. He has become the Door through which we are entering a new era of our salvation. It is an era of advancing the Kingdom by watching with Him in prayer together. When the glory of the Lord came to Ezekiel as he was by the river Chebar it was for the purpose of establishing him as a watchman of God in his generation. As Ezekiel experienced the glory, his destiny became crystal clear. God's priorities became Ezekiel's priorities. God's perspective became Ezekiel's perspective. God's Word became Ezekiel's word. God's strength became Ezekiel's strength. And God's victory became Ezekiel's victory.

...Brightness everywhere! The way a rainbow springs out of the sky on a rainy day—that's what it was like. It turned out to be the Glory of God! When I saw all this, I fell to my knees, my face to the ground. Then I heard a voice. It said, "Son of man, stand up. I have something to say to you."... "Tell them, 'This is the Message of God, the Master.' They are a defiant bunch. Whether or not they listen, at least they'll know that a prophet's been here....Only take care, son of man, that you don't rebel like these rebels. Open your mouth and eat what I give you" (Ezekiel 1:27-28; 2:1,4-5,8 TM).

God is calling us near. The Son is building His Father's house. Every Christian has a part in this exciting and glorious work. We are repairing the altar of God in the earth that He might come down in demonstration of His light and glory as in days of old. The altar begins in our hearts and moves out to the corporate demonstration of His Body which has been set in order.

The part each man contributes does not arise from what many call "individualism" or personal opinion. It comes from our reflection of particular facets of His glory. Christ is being formed in us, and we are reflecting His glory. Together we form majestic gemstones, each one multifaceted, flashing out Christ's brilliance as we turn before the eyes of the world. We are reflecting the glory of God, not creating our own self-expression. Throughout His life on earth, Jesus said, "I honor my Father; I do not seek My own glory."

As we restore a foundation of honor, we will build the altar upon which God will bring visitation and victory (see Rev. 21:2-3, 10-12,14; 22:14-15). To restore a foundation of honor, we need to show honor with our lips and with our actions.

What do we honor? Take a look at what the Bible tells us to honor:

1. Honor God in His commandments (see Deut. 30:15-16).

2. Honor the Bible (see Ps. 138:2).

3. Honor the name, *Jesus Christ* (see Acts 4:10-12).

4. Honor the Holy Spirit (see Acts 2:38-39).

5. Honor one another (see Phil. 2:3-4).

6. Honor your bodies (see 1 Cor. 6:19-20).

7. Honor work (see 1 Thess. 4:11-12).

8. Honor the Church (see 2 Cor. 8:23).

9. Honor your father and mother (see Eph.6:2).

10. Honor Church fathers (see Heb. 13:17).

11. Honor liberty (see Gal. 5:1,13-14).

12. Honor the forefathers (see Gen. 18:17-19).

We could preach a sermon on any one of these things. Which one of them stands out to you?

How can you show more honor in a particular way—and thereby increase the honor and reverence you show to your holy God?

MOUNTAIN OF PRAYER

When Jesus was transfigured on the mountain, He had taken the same disciples with him who regularly watched with Him in prayer (see Matt. 17, Mark 9, and Luke 9). They spent the night with Him on the mountain as they regularly did. But this time something different happened. Jesus showed them His glory and Heaven came down. They saw that the greatest champions of God from olden days were still alive and that they knew about God's plans for the world. God had a reason for catching them up in the ecstasy of that moment. In that moment they knew that truly Jesus held all authority over the earth, and that they were to be part of the master plan.

God is calling us to the mountain of the prayer of His Presence in these days so He can show us His glory. He wants us to truly see Him that we may also be changed, commissioned, and equipped to go out and fulfill His mission in the earth.

God wants us to clap our hands more than we ever did before. God wants us to shout in the anointing as never before. God wants us to sing with a loud noise, and dance as we honor His name. He will get us deeper into the revelation of His name. When we honor and worship the name of Jesus, we find ourselves on holy ground. We welcome the Holy Ghost, we run in freedom, we cry, and shout, all out of a reverence for this wonderful holy Lord.

When we get into revival, reverence comes. When we show reverence, the glory comes. When the glory comes, we will enter into His victory every time. In His Presence we are on holy ground.

As we are awakened to the presence of the Lord in the mountain of prayer, it is all too inviting to want to hole up there in glorious ecstasy. But, in fact, we see that God reveals Himself to us in prayer that He may inhabit us and send us down from the mountain out into the world to take our place as watchmen on the walls for our families, our churches, our cities, our nations, and our world. From the place of intimate fellowship, deep calls unto deep and we hear the voice of the Master, "Who will go for us?" As our hearts respond to His awakening surely we must answer, "Lord, I'll go. Holy is Your name!"

CHAPTER 3

Set the World Right

Your Kingdom Come...

RECOGNIZING THE SET INTENTION OF GOD FOR THE EARTH.

The 1977 movie, *Close Encounters of the Third Kind*, is the story of a simple man who begins to realize he has been invited into a world much bigger than his small private life. Electrical lineman Roy Neary is just an everyday guy, but his normal life collapses when he becomes obsessed with finding out the meaning of the messages he is receiving. Roy embarks on a journey that climaxes on a mountain where well-intentioned alien beings meet humans from earth. When he arrives, he finds people from every nation and language have been called out as he has. The communication between the space inhabitants and earth is a simple pattern of five musical tones played in sequence. As the scientists begin sending back the "song" they are receiving from the heavens, a huge craft suddenly appears and sings back. It blows the facility power supply to smithereens. But the whole test area breaks into jubilation as contact becomes reality.

When we wake up to harmony with Heaven through a life of unceasing prayer, we make contact with the throne from which all things temporary and eternal flow. More than that, we begin a duet with the One who sits on that throne and holds all things together by the Word of His power. Our simple, ordinary lives become extraordinary as He invites us into a participating role that reaches beyond our private lives.

The simple prayer of faith draws Heaven down. There are few things to compare with the jubilation of the reality that God listens to our words. When He speaks back, the great power of His voice moves the earth. These "close encounters" are what we are looking for.

When the earliest Christians prayed standing up, with their faces open toward Heaven and their arms outstretched in expectation, they were not praying in vain. By going faithfully into the Holy Place, Zechariah had a close encounter with an angel of Heaven. When Anna and Simeon, who daily prayed to God in His temple, came to pray one particular morning, they had a close encounter with the One whose coming they had been watching for.[1] Watching in prayer sets an atmosphere for ongoing close encounters with the Lord of Glory.

HEAVEN TO EARTH

When we pray "Your Kingdom come," we are praying Heaven down to earth.

The first thing we recognize about God's Kingdom is His absolute supremacy and power as Lord over all. When we pray, "Your Kingdom come," we are making ourselves His subjects. That means we acquiesce to become the servants of His will and plan.

When we pray, "Your Kingdom come," we are moving from passive to aggressive. We become the violent ones who advance the Kingdom by force of His power. *"From the days of John the Baptist until now the kingdom of heaven suffers violence, and the violent take it by force"* (Matt. 11:12).

Those who watch in prayer are going back to the origin of humankind and, as the offspring of the Last Adam, they are resuming the high call of being created in God's image. Watchers accept and take up again the charge to tend and watch the garden of God while uprooting the garden of satan, which is in chaos and darkness. It was God's original intention that the garden He planted be tended by the man made in His image. But failing the command to watch as well as tend, Adam and his wife fell to temptation. This failure is echoed in Jesus' words to His disciples in Gethsemane, where He told them to watch and pray lest they also fall into temptation to desert and betray Him. Had the first watchman (Adam) been vigilant, he would have grabbed the devil by the scruff of his slimy neck during that fatal controversy with Eve, and tossed him out of the garden on his ear!

Nebuchadnezzar was the ruler of the world when God gave him a revelation of the true King as he lay in his bed one night. In Nebuchadnezzar's dream, he saw that there are spiritual realities conducting spiritual activities that are invisible to the naked eye. He saw watchers, majestic messengers of Heaven bringing decrees from the throne of God that concerned the kingdoms of this earth:

> *I saw in the visions of my head while on my bed, and there was a watcher, a holy one, coming down from heaven. He cried aloud and said thus: "…This decision is by decree of the watchers, and the sentence by the word of the holy ones, in order that the living may know that the Most High rules in the kingdom of men, gives it to whomever He will, and sets over it the lowest of men"* (Daniel 4:13,14,17).

The watcher told the king that his sovereignty would be removed until he recognized God rules over the realm of humankind and sets up rulers as He wishes. When Nebuchadnezzar heard the decree he realized he was not in charge. He also learned that holy messengers participate in administering the Kingdom of Heaven on earth.

The Church enters into that work as, one by one, our hearts are awakened to fulfill our priestly ministry together as intercessors. In these latter days, the Church has become the chosen vessel to carry the Kingdom to the earth.

In giving his defense, the first Christian martyr, Stephen, testified to the Sanhedrin that the congregation of Israel had been ordained to be a testimony of the heavenly Kingdom as they dwelt among the kingdoms of men. Every land they entered, every earthly king that heard of them would also hear that the greatest King ruled earth from His throne in Heaven. *"Heaven is my throne and earth is my footstool"* (Isa. 66:1; see also Matt. 5:35).

Called Out

Jesus said, *"On this rock I will build My church and the gates of Hades shall not prevail against it"* (Matt. 16:18). The word that Jesus used in this first mention of the church is the Greek word, *ekklesia*. It literally means, "the called out ones." In that day and age, this was the term used to denote the governing authority, those called out to judge and govern the people. This is where we get the idea that the Church is not just an assembly of people, but also a *ruling body of believers*, founded on the revelation that the Rock, Jesus Christ, to whom and through whom all authority in Heaven and earth has been given, reigns and rules on the earth.

The main activity immediately coupled with Jesus' first mention of the Church is authority to bring the Kingdom of Heaven to earth through the activity of prayer—*"I will give you the keys of the kingdom of heaven, and whatever you bind on earth will be bound in heaven, and whatever you loose on earth will be loosed in heaven"* (Matt. 16:19). The Church is the vehicle through which

God advances His Kingdom. Prayer and the proclamation of the Gospel are the means by which we will prevail. *"...Now the manifold wisdom of God might be made known by the church to the principalities and powers in heavenly places"* (Eph. 3:10).

In Judaism, there are certain prayers that cannot be uttered unless there is at least a *minyan* ("count," or quorum) of ten believers gathered together in agreement. A *minyan* is also necessary for any public worship. In the Hebraic tradition, one's spirituality is never solely an individual affair; it is always experienced in the framework of a larger community.

What we see on Pentecost is the glory and presence of God through the Holy Spirit, and the context in which He appears is in the corporate gathering of the Church, watching and praying in one accord. The Church born under the heel of a pagan society, opposed by the might of the Roman Empire, and powerless in its own right, this small band of 120, began to vibrate with the power and glory of the Kingdom and turned the kingdoms of the world upside down in a matter of generations. They accomplished this through corporate watching together in prayer.

Stretched Out

In the early Church the power of the corporate body watching and praying in one accord was the key to the release of what we define as the apostolic ministry: preaching the Gospel with signs, wonders, and miracles.

We find that many people want to be part of an apostolic church. They say, "We are apostolic." And yet, they don't give much attention to the Scriptures such as the ones in which Paul the apostle (who is a type of an apostolic church) wrote: "I proved myself with fastings often, in watchings often" (see 2 Cor. 11:26-28). People don't want to know the part of the apostolic package that involves fasting and watching. Of course, when Paul talks about watchings, it is in the context of watching and praying.

Part of the apostolic release of the end-time Church, we believe, will be a grace for watching in prayer. Signs and wonders and the outpouring of the Holy Spirit are there for us, but they come in the context of the preached Word and standing in intercession for our families, our churches, our cities. We must learn to be watchmen. God calls the people of the Church to become watchmen on the walls and the more corporate we become, the better it is. There is more power in corporate watching and praying.

We find an extraordinary example of this in the story of Peter's miraculous release from prison in Acts 12: *"Peter was therefore kept in prison, but constant prayer was offered to God for him by the church"* (Acts 12:5). Peter's plight was dire, but notice that *he was not praying*—he was *sleeping*. It was the Spirit-filled Church that had the mission, through prayer and prayer alone, to rescue him from this perilous situation. They understood that they had access to a Kingdom authority that was greater than any held by the earthly and spiritual rulers of that age. The Church engaged in constant, watching prayer. They were a picture of apostolic prayer: fervent, continuous, unswayed by circumstances or disappointments, prevailing until the victory is won.

They did not pray a few hours one day, but a long time. It says they offered "constant prayer." By the time of Peter's rescue, they may have been engaged for several if not many days of prayer already. Even in the middle of the night, there were some who were gathered together in watching prayer for Peter's life.

Watching prayer was not new to those first Christians. They came from a long tradition of watching through the night in prayer for deliverance from their enemies. It began with the first Passover as Hebrew slaves slaughtered the lamb and put the blood on the doorframe of their homes. God told them to clothe themselves in preparation for their deliverance. They ate the covenant meal and stayed awake in prayer and expectation as God had instructed. Just as He promised, while they watched and waited, in great signs and wonders His deliverance came. Every year since that time, on the eve of Passover, Jews around the world keep the watch vigil. Since that very first watch the attitude of an awakened posture of prayer expressed by staying up through the night hours in expectation of the coming of Messiah has become a lifestyle for many descendants of Abraham. David is considered one of their watchmen. His psalms are full of references to prayer, worship and meditation on the Word of God during the night hours. *"At midnight I will rise to give thanks to You..."* (Ps. 119:62). After their last supper together on the Eve of Passover in Jerusalem, Jesus took several friends with Him to keep the watch together. While He knew his mission, the friends were unaware and fell asleep in that crucial hour. Watching in prayer has always been a strategic corporate spiritual event. It remains today for the followers of Christ. As we have said, He is once again in the garden under the olives. In this hour He will not be alone.

After days and nights of constant prayer, suddenly, an angel of the Lord appeared to Peter and the prison cell was filled with a bright light. Apostolic prayer *will* move Heaven and earth, releasing angels to hearken to His Word. The angel, who had just come from the very presence of God, carried the Shekinah glory of that presence when he came.

This glory-light is equation-changing. We've seen it and experienced it. It's alive. It comes from the Presence, from Heaven. And it changes the equations on earth when it arrives. When we pray, "Your Kingdom come," we are inviting Heaven's light to shine into the darkness.

Deliverance comes in the glory light. The angel struck Peter to wake him up, and Peter's chains fell off. In the same way, our corporate, fervent prayers will loose chains of iniquity, injustice, darkness, and oppression and release captives to freedom. The account also gives us a picture of the power of prayer to loose the Church to her destiny—a Church bound by religion, humanism, and principalities of this age; chained between soldiers; imprisoned by iron gates; but set free by prayer.

The more we get in the glory and in prayer, the more we guarantee that chains are going to fall off. Yokes and chains are going to fall off of our family members, of our communities, off of our cities, and off of nations as we press into His glory in watching prayer.

Peter was led by the angel through the gates and past the guard posts. The city gate opened of its own accord. Jesus, you will remember, said that he was going to build His Church and the gates of hell would not prevail against it (see Matthew 16:18). No matter what the enemy has thrown at you, no matter what gates of iron may seem to block your path, this is the promise to the Church of Jesus Christ.

Peter arrived at the house of Mary, the mother of John Mark, *"where many were gathered together praying"* (Acts 12:12). Here the Church is defined as more than just those who have personally applied the blood of Jesus to their lives. The continuing activities of receiving apostolic instruction, fellowship, communion, and prayer all prove to be vital for the Church to grow from a loose-knit posse to an *ekklesia*, a body of those who govern together in Kingdom authority, led by the Spirit and subject to the Head.

The word translated as "constant" or "earnest" prayer in this passage is the Greek word *ektenes,* which means "stretched out." It connotes stretched out both in terms of a long time and, more importantly, in terms of souls being stretched out in the intensity of earnestness toward God. Jesus prayed like this in the garden as He kept watch on the night that He was betrayed, "Jesus prayed earnestly" (see Luke 22:44). That's one of the keys to apostolic authority in prayer: Stretch out all the way to get God's presence.

The caveat is that in our earnestness and fervency, we remain in the anointing, that we don't strive in the flesh, but that we watch and pray *in the Spirit*.

Corporate watching prayer is God's awesome secret weapon. Personal devotion, personal praise, and prayer are powerful, but the corporate body harmonizing in prayer and apostolic intercession releases authority to see cities taken overnight. I believe the end-time believing Church is on a rescue operation for millions of souls. We are on a rescue operation for our nation to come into revival. We are on a rescue operation for all the members of our family to be saved. We are on a rescue operation to see signs and wonders and the greater works restored to His Church, to confirm the Gospel message.

Walking Out

The watchman goes beyond building a bridge between Heaven and earth in prayer. Watchmen become the bridge over which Jesus walks. The very meaning of *intercession* is to be the one who stands in the broken-down place between God and man and makes up the gap. In a sense, with one hand we grasp the hand of God and with the other, we hold tight to the failing hand of man. A beautiful example of this took place in the life of Monica, a member of our community of faith. Here is Monica's story:

> I was born on December 25, and my parents' first names were José and María, Spanish for Joseph and Mary. Despite these Christian names, my parents were not Christians of any denomination. A few years ago, my mother came to Christ, but my father had no interest in Christianity. He was estranged from the rest of the family because

of his alcoholism and abusive behavior. Because he lived elsewhere and had no telephone, I had no way of contacting him and we had not spoken for over seven years.

In late 2007 at a Sunday service, Pastor Chavda called the women who had felt rejected by their fathers to come forward for prayer. I did so, and Pastor Chavda both prayed and encouraged me to believe that God had something in store for me. Soon after that, on Christmas Day, I called my mother and sister. They were not home, but to my surprise, my father was visiting them, and we were able to talk. I was able to tell him I loved him, and I could tell that he was softer than normal. Then my husband was able to speak to him. One thing led to another, and then, to my astonishment, he was soon praying the sinner's prayer, asking Jesus Christ to become his Lord and Savior. What a Christmas-birthday present for me!

Our whole family of faith remembers many Friday nights at The Watch where Monica stood as a watchman for her family. From that glorious Christmas day when her father prayed to receive the gift of Christ, until now, his joy is her joy, her joy is our joy, and our joy is the joy of Jesus.

Apostolic intercession will never give up, with fasted determination we will keep on walking it out. We will keep on praying.

How Long?

As the Church in the latter days, we are just on the border of revival. We are envisioning a revival that crosses international borders and ethnic lines, reaches over denominational walls and strikes the heart of darkness to bring out the slaves of sin. We are praying apostolically and expectantly for a spiritual earthquake that will be off the Richter scale!

How long will we pray for revival? Until it comes. For our families, for our churches, for our nations, for Israel and for Jerusalem, we will pray until it comes.

In James 4:2 we read these words: "You do not have because you do not ask." George Müller said,

> It is not enough to begin to pray, nor to pray aright; nor is it enough to continue for a time to pray; but we must patiently believingly, continue in prayer until we obtain an answer; and further we have not only to continue in prayer unto the end, but we have also to believe that God does hear us, and will answer our prayers. Most frequently we fail in not continuing in prayer until the blessing is obtained, and in not expecting the blessing."[2]

The vigilant and joyful posture of watching in prayer is the core identity of Christianity. The essence of this posture is the expectation of the answer. And that answer is "yes" in Jesus Christ (see 2 Cor. 1:20). There is one ark of rescue, one refuge of hope designed and built by God for families around the world to run to for deliverance. That ark of safety is His Church. A revival of watching in prayer, particularly corporately, whether it is by twos and threes or by tens, dozens and hundreds can renew the light from God's lamp within "the city set on a hill." People may stop your polemics or preaching or politics, but your praying cannot be bound.

A Heritage of Watching

The Christian heritage of watching in prayer goes deep:

[T]he ideal of the more frequent prayer and of almost constant meditation on the Law was repeatedly set forth before the minds of fervent Jews by the psalms, especially Ps. 119. The psalms exerted an influence on the spirituality of the people of Israel that extended far beyond the matter of ritual prayer; they were also the object of religious teaching and personal meditation.

It was out of this praying people that Jesus Christ emerged.[3]

A glimpse into early Christian community reveals the unbound desire to watch and pray. Birthed out of the Jewish rhythms of daily prayers in the temple, the first Christians followed in the footsteps of the Master and His early apostles. Armed with the Old Testament Scriptures, Jewish Christians stood with their faces raised toward Heaven, praying with full expectation of the *parousia* (Second Coming) of Jesus. We see their shadows, palms up, arms stretched out in the pattern of the Cross, etched on the walls of the Palatine Hill, in the caves of the catacombs, and in mosaic relief from Jerusalem to Rome.

When the temple in Jerusalem was razed by Roman occupiers, prayer escaped. Offered five times a day, prayer followed the rhythms of human life. Retiring at nightfall and rising with the dawn, people continued to commune with God in prayer as receiving from Him the breath of His Spirit of life and ultimately exhaling back to Him in death with the assurance of the resurrection. That prayer is the evening prayer prayed by devout Jews as the last prayer of every day just before sleep. It is the prayer in expectation of rising with the dawn. This pattern of expectation is the prayer of Jesus from the Cross: "Into Your hands I commend My spirit." It was the ultimate prayer of victory as Christ gave up His last breath in full assurance of the Father's deliverance from the last enemy, death. Jesus knew He would awaken and rise from the grave.

It is in expectation of that ultimate victory we watch in prayer until He comes. Just as morning calls to mind the resurrection of Christ, evening recalls His passion. Just as the light of the sun overwhelms the dark of night, evening is the time of lighting of the lamps. This is the story of the oil given us by the Bridegroom in the parable of the virgins. Evening is the hour when work is finished and rest is entered into. It is the hour when lamps are lit to stay the darkness of night. It is the hour of returning home, to table and family.

As David offered in Psalms 141:2: *"Let my prayer be set forth before Thee as incense; and the lifting up of my hands as the evening sacrifice"* (KJV). Certainly Paul would have had this in mind, taken from the example of the apostolic community of Jesus, when he instructed his son Timothy to build the church:

> *Therefore I exhort first of all that supplications, prayers, intercessions, and giving of thanks be made for all men, for kings and all who are in authority, that we may lead a quiet and peaceable life in all godliness and reverence. For this is good and acceptable in the sight of God our Savior, who desires all men to be saved and to come to the knowledge of the truth. For there is one God and one Mediator between God and men, the Man Christ Jesus, who gave Himself a ransom for all, to be testified in due time....I desire therefore that men pray everywhere, lifting up holy hands, without wrath and doubting;* (1 Timothy 2:1-6,8).

Jesus began his final push in prayer in the garden as He lifted up hands in advance of His passion. The evening sacrifice, offered up the following day, was going to be He Himself. He took others with Him to participate in this offering. The evening sacrifice in the temple at which time Jews, wherever they were, would pause at the sound of the shofar from the temple, was the shadow of the true evening sacrifice of Christ on the Cross. The "lifting up of my hands" recalls the action of Jesus as He stretched out His hands to be nailed to Calvary. The evening sacrifice ultimately became the liturgical form of evensong.

The rhythms of prayer without ceasing had always erupted in the daily walk of Jesus; we hear Him break into prayer in the course of regular and irregular events. We know from His example that He was in constant fellowship with the Father and that out of that union He voiced the conversation they were carrying on. But He devoted Himself to corporate prayers in regular rhythms as well; the habit of His life would have been a reflection of the Jewish custom where prayer was kept in public, corporate worship five times a day. This pattern was observed into the seventh century throughout Arabia, wherever the Church went, from which Islam has adopted its ritual of bowing down five times a day wherever men are working or at leisure.

Imagine the power of unbound prayer if the Church turned again to the ways of our forefathers and recaptured their devotion to watching in prayer as the frontline of God's Kingdom advances.

Praying in Community

God has revealed Himself to be a community of persons, Father, Son and Holy Spirit, and has determined to bring us into His own life through the corporate life of His Body, the Church. "The witness of a God who is three and yet one speaks profoundly to our situation—not of an annihilation of the personal being, but of the fulfillment of personal being through relationship with others, through relationship to the Godhead."[4]

We are given several lights by which to gauge our spiritual bearings, including the foundation of Scripture and the voice of the Holy Spirit. He did not design us to live in isolation, but rather in community. We can only find our spiritual bearings as we relate to and are submitted to Christ's body, the Church, which is the origin, the beginning and the completion of the Christian's human experience of God and of Christ being formed in us. For a believer, community is essential for healthy Christian growth.

In the wake of 9-11, the Barna Research Group did a study on spirituality in America.[5] They found that while spiritual interest and church attendance surged dramatically after the terrorist attacks, within one year, trends in spiritual interest and practice receded to lower levels than before the attacks. While most people in America profess to be of the Christian faith, the research group found that if these American "Christians" attend church at all, 40 percent of them are religious homeless, nomads wandering from church to church. Of these nomads, 29 percent will change churches within one year and another 20 percent will rotate their church membership simultaneously among more than one congregation without fully identifying with any of them.

Too many Christians view church membership as optional, something that men have devised for pragmatic reasons having nothing to do with the requirements of Scripture. One often hears statements like, "The Bible does not tell me to join a church." "Having to belong to a church is legalistic." "Church is only there because men want to control people or get their money." "I don't believe in the institutional church. I worship at home." "My relationship with God is my private business. Being in public worship only hampers my relationship with my Savior." "I belong to the whole church, the spiritual universal church. I don't need to be part of a local church." "I'm too busy to be involved in a local church right now."

Jesus said that people cannot love God whom they do not see if they do not love other people, whom they do see. In the same way, your participation in the church local is the direct expression of your true relationship with the Church universal and it ultimately reflects your personal relationship with God Himself. Church membership is expected in the New Testament. The spiritual Church universal is the sum of local church bodies operating under the headship of Christ. All professing Christians need to seek out and join a church that preaches the true Gospel, administers the sacraments, exercises church discipline, and worships God in spirit and in truth.

Look at this "snapshot" of life in the early church. Justin Martyr, an early church father wrote in about the year A.D. 150:

> And on the day called Sunday all who live in the city or in the country gather together to one place and the memoirs of the apostles or the writings of the prophets are read, as long as time permits; then, when the reader has ceased, the president verbally instructs and exhorts to the imitation of these good things. Then we all rise together and pray, and...when our prayer is ended, bread and wine and water are brought, and the president in like manner offers prayers and thanksgivings according to his ability and the people assent saying Amen....And they who are well to do and willing, give what each thinks fit, and what is collected is deposited with the president who succors the orphans and widows and those in sickness or want, the prisoners and the strangers among us.[6]

Early Christians prayed often and long. As we have already mentioned, their typical physical position for prayer was face-up, alert and expectant. They instituted *"vigils,"* essentially prayer-watches, the chief of which occurred during Passion Week (the week before Easter). Earlier, the apostles had learned how to "pray through" from the example Jesus gave them. Remember the woman who contended for her daughter's healing? She refused to turn back even when Jesus suggested she might be like a "dog." Several times the New Testament letters to the churches report the Church fathers "striving in prayer" for the saints according to the will of God. These examples reveal the place of the watchman who is willing to grasp the will of God in Heaven and pull with all his spiritual force to bring the out-of-sync earth into harmony with it.

Such a posture of prevailing prayer is the backbone of faith and action in every generation, in every nation, in every heart, for every situation where Christ shall raise the tabernacle of David and fill His house of prayer with the incense of hearts revived. Watching in prayer is prayer moving beyond ourselves to the community, and beyond the community to the world. Watchmen move beyond the present moment into the economy of future salvation.

The seventeenth chapter of John's Gospel is the longest prayer in the Bible. It's the high priestly prayer of Jesus, and it follows the Levitical pattern for the day of atonement described in Leviticus chapter 16. After Jesus presented Himself to the Father, He prayed, "...for those You gave Me out of the world" (see John 17:6). Jesus prayed for His disciples who were obedient to Him and who kept His Word. He acknowledged that their security rests in the unity of their hearts with His. This ongoing harmony will bind them to Him and to His will after He has ascended into Heaven. The focus of His prayer for His friends was for the ongoing work of sanctification that the Word and the Spirit will create in them. Jesus ended His prayer with the personal seal with which God signs all of His work: *"That the love with which You loved Me may be in them, and I in them"* (John 17:26).

Jesus prays us into the "community" of Father, Son, and Holy Spirit.

To the Mountain

Jesus went, as was His custom, into the mountain to pray during the night watches (see Luke 22:39). Apparently, He usually would take with Him two or three of His watchmen friends, most often James, John, and Peter. Watching was commanded by God in keeping with the observance of Passover. That is where the spiritual concept originates. Jesus kept this observance as a regular way of prayer.

It was this kind of prayer, prayer to effect salvation for the world, which caught the imagination of Jesus' closest friends. As they watched His style they said, "Teach us." We are learning from the Master, who told us to keep vigil with Him.

We are taking back the night. We are reclaiming the territory formerly possessed by the early Church, prevailing in corporate prayer. While the world sleeps, the watchmen are awake, routing the enemy, delivering the captives, and taking away the spoils of his kingdom.

"Your Kingdom come," the prayer of the apostolic Church, is a corporate expression. Individually and corporately we stretch ourselves out in prayer in a posture of expectation until Christ comes. We will fulfill what Jesus asked when He said in the Gospels, *What I say to you, I say to all: Watch!"* (Mark 13:37).

The final amen to all Christian praying from the days of those first apostles onward is the appearing of the Lord Jesus Christ. All Christian prayer prevails in the expectation of His appearing. We are praying toward the consummation of His will, which is His Kingdom established and a new Heaven, a new earth, filled with His new creation.

ENDNOTES

1. See Luke 1:8-20 and Luke 2:25-38.

2. D.M. McIntyre, *The Hidden Life of Prayer* (London: Marshall, Morgan & Scott, n.d.), 86.

3. A.G. Martimort, I.H. Dalmais, P. Jounel, eds., *The Church at Prayer: Liturgy and Time* (Collegeville, MN: Liturgical Press, 1986) 160. (Translated from the French.)

4. Ralph Martin, *Hungry for God: Practical Help in Personal Prayer* (Ann Arbor, MI: Servant Publications, 2006) 31.

5. The Barna Group, "Half of All Adults Say Their Faith Helped Them Personally Handle the 9-11 Aftermath," (The Barna Update, Sept. 3, 2002); http://www.barna. org/FlexPage.aspx?Page=BarnaUpdate&BarnaUpdateI D=120

6. Justin Martyr, *The First Apology,* quoted in Robert A. Baker and John M. Landers, *A Summary of Christian History* (Nashville: B&H Publishing Group, 2005), 15.

CHAPTER 4

Do What's Best

...*Your Will Be Done*...

ACTIVATING WHAT IS SETTLED IN HEAVEN AND LOOSING IT ON THE EARTH.

Two days after Christmas, I (Bonnie) got a call that my mother, who had been suffering from multiple sclerosis, had taken a turn for the worse and they were calling the family to come to her bedside. In our years of preaching the Gospel, Mahesh and I have seen literally thousands of instantaneous miraculous healings, from Stage IV cancers to AIDS. My mother had always been in our prayers, but God didn't heal my mother in that way. Over the years we had witnessed her physical body being progressively taken in the grip of that disease. But as she lost control of her limbs and body, and even her speech and ability to communicate diminished, her spirit and her faith did not waiver for a second. Through the years, she remained full of faith and expectation.

I remember that from the time that I was a young child that my mother would go back, on a weekly and sometimes a daily basis, to one Scripture that she had underlined in her Bible. It was from First Corinthians 13, that great chapter on love. She lived this passage. Everywhere, she exuded the aroma of Christ. And at the end of her life, her testimony to all those who knew her was that she was the kindest, most patient, gentle, long-suffering, unselfish person. Her one mission was that all of her friends, family, loved ones and especially her children and grandchildren, would know the Lord as their Savior. She accomplished her mission.

Her favorite poem was "Stopping by Woods on a Snowy Evening," by Robert Frost.

Whose woods these are I think I know.
His house is in the village though;
He will not see me stopping here
To watch his woods fill up with snow.
My little horse must think it queer
To stop without a farmhouse near
Between the woods and frozen lake
The darkest evening of the year.
He gives his harness bells a shake
To ask if there is some mistake.
The only other sound's the sweep
Of easy wind and downy flake.
The woods are lovely, dark and deep.
But I have promises to keep,
And miles to go before I sleep,
And miles to go before I sleep.

This poem had become a parable of her life; she had stopped in the "woods" of this mortal life for a season, but at a certain point, it was appointed for her to go on in to the promises of God. As I read the poem to my mother one last time, I got to the lines, "...I have promises to keep," and miles to go before I sleep." Mom, unable to speak, nodded her head.

Our family kept vigil around the clock as we watched her enter what they call the throes of death. But, in the face of that momentary reality, there was another law at work. As her body weakened and she slipped into a coma, the glory of the Lord began to fill the room. It was evident to all—His personal presence and friendship, a sense of time and space and the kingdoms of this world opening and being filled with His manifest presence. In her last hours, she suddenly awoke from her coma as if from a dream, her eyes wide open and full of anticipation. She had been unable to control her body for years, but in this moment she raised up off the bed and stretched out her arms, a look of joy and encounter on her face as she greeted someone whom we could not see with our natural eyes. We looked at her and looked around to see who it was, and then we began to cry with joy as we witnessed another law at work, the law of the One who said, "I was dead, but am alive forever more." It lasted for just a moment, and then she resumed the deep sleep of a coma.

As we gathered around her bed, we sang psalms and her favorite hymns to her, and we read to her from Scripture, the great salvation promises and all about the glory of the resurrection and eternal life. I heard myself, as I stretched out my hand toward her, blessing and commending this mortal creation to her new and glorious body, a body without disease, where there is no more sting of death. I thanked her for her life, the race that she had run with faithfulness, and her mission accomplished.

As we had watched her for years and had prayed for years that God would raise her up, we suddenly realized that all of our prayers were coming true before our eyes, that He indeed was raising her up—into a new body, in a new life.

I prayed a simple prayer, "Lord Jesus in Your mercy, come now and embrace Mom." It was as though the Lord stepped into the room in a dance. With the sheer presence of His eternal glory, He moved sorrow. He moved sadness. He moved despair. And He moved death. My mother took three peaceful breaths, and her mortal flesh slipped into sleep. We began to worship and respond to the King of glory. Christ had conquered all evil. His will had been done.

The following Monday we awoke to find a gentle snow falling that continued to fall and blanket the land in white as we gathered to celebrate my mother's memorial service. It was a sign that indeed heaven was touching earth with the glory of God in answer to our prayers even in the face of death.

PRAYING THE WILL OF GOD

As we began this writing, we were guests in the home of friends who told us of a time when they prayed the will of God. In 1984, Leslie's mother was dying of pancreatic cancer and Leslie was pleading with God to spare her, as she was only 61 years old. As Leslie was walking back and forth on her front porch she asked the Lord, "How should I pray for my mother?"

Immediately she heard, "My will be done."

"What?" she responded.

Again she heard, "Pray, 'My will be done.'"

Leslie said, "OK—Your will be done." She reports that as she prayed that simple prayer, a burden was lifted off her spirit, and she felt the peace of the Lord. Continuing to pray that prayer over the weeks that followed, and embracing the will of God even if it meant He would say "no" to her request for healing, Leslie was not dismayed when, about a month later, her mother passed on to be with the Lord.

On the basis of the finished work of Calvary and the example of Jesus' healing ministry we know for certain that the will of God is our deliverance from oppression, peace from torment, forgiveness of sin, and healing from disease (see Isa. 53). God has one consistent nature. He is the same today as when He delivered and healed in the Old Testament and as He delivered and healed in the New. Christ became "poor that we might be made rich." Therefore when we pray, "Your will be done," we pray in full faith and expectancy of deliverance, peace, forgiveness, and healing.

The glory that all of us experienced in the presence of these homegoings was the same sweet answer to prayers which we celebrate when someone is healed of cancer.

Not a Passive Prayer

When you pray, "Your will be done," it is not a passive prayer. It is activating what is settled in Heaven and loosing it on the earth.

Now this is the confidence that we have in Him, that if we ask anything according to His will, He hears us. And if we know that He hears us, whatever we ask, we know that we have the petitions that we have asked of Him (1 John 5:14-15).

Many of us have had that dreaded experience of being in a crisis situation in which someone offers the less-than-helpful prayer, "Lord help us, *if it be Thy will.*" If it be His will? Of course God has a will, and it is His will to help us. It's just that we don't always know what His will looks like. His will is to see the whole of creation dancing to the song of life coming from the throne. In praying, "Your will be done," we align ourselves with God's divine intent. We amen His desires for our world. We ask Him to "Do what's best."

God's throne is a throne of judgment. His judgment is something that we tend to avoid at all costs, but perhaps we've been looking through the dark glasses of religion and haven't seen the glory of God in true judgment. One cannot experience true love except when judgment is involved. In true love, we love someone even though we know them completely. We know what's right with them and we know what's wrong with them, and we delight in being related to them permanently in the face of this true judgment. The majesty of God's judgment is that He knows us entirely and loves us ardently and completely. And it is His will to do so.

The second face of God's majestic judgment is justice. The Bible says that the foundations of His throne are righteousness and justice. In other words, justice is also the will of God. When you think of the ultimate wrongs committed against persons you may love, justice is sweet. A child who has been abused or worse, whole populations that have been terrorized and oppressed, races against whom genocide has been committed, these things call for justice.

Christ bore the judgment of God's wrath on the Cross. That act allows all who receive Him to escape the final penalty for sin and it looses God's justice. The Lamb who takes away the sins of the world speaks to us of God's will regarding justice:

For as the Father has life in Himself, so He has granted the Son to have life in Himself, and has given Him authority to execute judgment also, because He is the Son of Man. Do not marvel at this; for the hour is coming in which all who are in the graves will hear His voice and come forth—those who have done good, to the resurrection of life, and those who have done evil, to the resurrection of condemnation. I can of Myself do nothing. As I hear, I judge; and My judgment is righteous, because I do not seek My own will but the will of the Father who sent Me (John 5:26-30).

It is in this context that we can understand that a prayer for His will to be done is not a passive prayer. We no longer pray, "if," but "that" God's will be done. Through Jesus' life, lived in the will of God and laid down at the Father's bidding, He broke into Heaven carrying us with Him. There, presently, Jesus watches and prays that the will of God be done in us on the earth until He comes again.

"Bend Me, Lord"

Prior to the Welsh Revival of 1904, a young man named Evan Roberts prayed a simple, fervent prayer: "Bend me, O Lord!"

One sunny day, as I (Bonnie) was finishing a book about revival with my assistant, Heather, I had just concluded typing the last sentence, "Your key to living in permanent revival: 'Bend me, Lord,'" and I clicked on "Save." Instantaneously, the clear, sunny day turned into a massive, raging rainstorm. A blinding downpour with flashes of lightning and thunder settled over our house for about three minutes. Heather and I wanted to crawl under the table. And then a wind came through our house, slamming and opening and closing doors.

Mahesh had been in the back of the house, studying, and he came out saying, "What is happening here?"

I said, "We just finished writing *100 Year Bloom* with Evan Roberts' prayer, 'Bend me, O Lord,' and this downpour and wind came. We think He likes it!"

It's part of His will for His people to bow to Him, surrender to His love, accept everything He wants to do. When we pray in accord with that, we can't go wrong!

Blessing the Government

When we pray in the Friday watch, we always pray for the governments of our country and others. Sometimes it can be difficult to know the will of God for your government. How should we pray when we can see so many wrong things happening?

Our mentor and friend, Derek Prince, used to tell about what happened to him during World War II when he was a British soldier serving in the Sudan. Rommel was getting ready to advance in Africa and the last line for defense in North Africa was the British army.

Derek got to the battlefield and found the troops in disarray. Drunken officers were using supplies for their own needs while men didn't even have enough water for their canteens in the hot desert. It was a mess. Derek had recently been saved and baptized in the Holy Spirit, so he said, "God, how do I pray?" And the Lord spoke to him and gave him this prayer: "Lord, give us leaders such that it would be to Your glory to give us the victory through them." That was a Holy Ghost prayer, completely within the will of God. Derek began to pray it.

Just days later, Derek said he was listening to the radio and a tremor and chill went through his body when a report came that the man the British high command had chosen to send to the battlefront to lead that defense had been instantly killed when his plane touched down; it had clipped its wing on the tarmac, flipped, and crashed. The British high command, in desperation, grabbed a man named Montgomery and sent him to the front.

Montgomery arrived at the front, took one look, and called everybody into the yard in public, officers and privates alike. He told them, "The whole world is depending on us but we have no strength for this battle. We are utterly dependent on God who gives victory in battle. Therefore, we are going to get our act together to keep covenant with Him." From that point forward, the victory was in the bag, Rommel's army was indeed defeated and the history of the world is different today because of it.

When you want to pray God's will for national and international affairs, ask the Holy Spirit. He will guide your prayers in the same way He guided Derek in that critical time in world history.

GETTING ON GOD'S AGENDA

True prayer is like slow-dancing with God. As He leads us and as our hearts are joined to His, our steps follow His. We come into alignment with His will. Being led means being governed by the Holy Spirit day to day, finding moment-to-moment fellowship with the Godhead. This opens a portal of His will into earth's realm and when we pray, "Your will be done!" down here, we end up praying exactly according to His will as He is enthroned up there.

In other words, in order to pray His will we must develop intimacy with the Father. One way to break through into intimacy is to establish a "dwelling place" for your prayers, some physical place you go to regularly. In such a place, you practice prayer and you experience that sensation of letting yourself go in God.

People tend to think that one cannot express this kind of intimate liberty in a corporate setting, but we see that Jesus regularly took His most intimate friends in to pray with Him, and together they experienced the transfiguration of harmonizing with the Father, watching in prayer together. This is the practical purpose of setting the watch and keeping it corporately.

When we pray "Your will be done" we plant our feet and hold the line against all that opposes His will—even when that means letting go of our own desires, opinions, ideas, and plans. It is clear that He ardently desires to hand the Kingdom to us; He demonstrated it on Calvary. It is His great pleasure to hand us this inheritance, sealed with the down payment of the gifts and power of the Holy Spirit. But in order to partake of His overcoming banquet in an ongoing way, the eater must also be willing to also "drink His cup."

When Jesus posed this challenge to His disciples He was speaking of His own death and signifying that all who follow Him will "hate" their own lives, meaning each one will take his cross daily for His sake.

The watchman has an eternal grasp on everyday life. The Gospel, the proclamation of it in fullness, and faithfulness to the Champion who gave it become top priority. The world, the flesh and the devil are all stubbornly autonomous from God. But when we walk with the One who conquered sin and death, we become those who are "led" by the Spirit. *"For if you live according to the flesh you will die; but if by the Spirit you put to death the deeds of the body, you will live. For as many as are led by the Spirit of God, these are the sons of God"* (Rom. 8:13-14).

The "led" ones are the mature sons of God. Mature sons of God do not continue in sin, which Derek Prince succinctly defined as "the problem of missing the will of the Father." In an article he wrote, he defined sin as, "an attitude of rebellion against God, a refusal to accept the righteous dominion of God, a refusal to say in every event and circumstance, 'thy will be done'"[1]

Thy Will—Or My Will?

Personal opinion has become politically sacred. Opinion, exalted on the dais of relativism, now holds as much importance as time-tested, immovable truths. The blogosphere has become hallowed ground.

In the Christian world, somehow Luther's propositions on the priesthood of all believers and the right of believers to read the Bible for themselves have been misconstrued, in many cases making us into little gods who claim sovereign rights to personal preferences on everything from sexuality to church affiliation. Mothering skills now must include seven-step negotiation protocols on how to handle your three-year-old who is thrashing about in the church foyer screaming at the top of his opinionated little lungs.

This "my will be done" atmosphere pervades the entire "civilized" world in this generation. Everyone demands the right to do what is right in his or her own eyes. It has swamped our theology. Our modern spirituality is created according to individual expression and impulse.

In his book, *Christianity's Dangerous Idea*, Alister McGrath proposes this:

> The "dangerous idea" lying at the heart of Protestantism is that the interpretation of the Bible is each individual's right and responsibility. The spread of this principle has resulted in five hundred years of remarkable innovation and adaptability, but it has also created cultural incoherence and social instability. Without any overarching authority to rein in "wayward" thought, opposing sides on controversial issues can only appeal to the Bible— yet the Bible is open to many diverse interpretations.[2]

In our world, people consider anything labeled "orthodox" or "sacred" or "traditional" suspect, as though nothing old could contain any wisdom or truth. This is one of the forces that we encounter as we attempt to pray according to God's will.

His will may not be the same as somebody's latest opinion about it. In fact, God's will often seems to be veiled and elusive.

More Questions Than Answers

Jesus expressed the will of His Father in His recorded words. But He also left plenty of room for discovery. In good Jewish form, Jesus asked a lot of questions—157 of them have been captured in the Gospels. His questions were often his answer to questions put to Him.

One of His questions, spoken to two men who were starting to follow Him, was, *"What do you seek?"* (John 1:38). It is a profound question, if you stop and think about it. What (or whom) do you search for? Why are you searching? How are you searching?

In J.R.R. Tolkien's *Lord of the Rings*, Gollum started out as a regular person in the Shire, but he turned into a pitiable and miserable creature through seeking the wrong thing. It's true that the Ring he sought was very important, but Gollum misappropriated the value of that ring for his own life and destiny. By focusing so hard on his own desire, he ended up losing his chief desire, which was not the Ring, but identity and glory.

Andrew and the other unnamed disciple answered Jesus' question with another question, *"Where are you staying?"* (John 1:38). They recognized that finding what they were seeking could take a while. They needed to abide with this man Jesus long enough to decide what He stood for. They needed to allow their desires and expectations to be formed in new ways. So do we.

What was Jesus' response? He said, *"Come and see"* (verse 39). They went with Him to where He was staying. You have to wonder what the conversation with Jesus was like around the table. These good Jews, who had been expecting the coming of this Messiah all of their lives, had not known what He would look like or what He would do when He came. When Jesus showed up, few people could tell that He was the One.

So often in our own lives the Lord may not necessarily show up as we were expecting. But when we ask Him where He's staying and He says, "Come and see," we will find out. We really do have to stay with Him even though some of our desires and ambitions and expectations may be circumvented or disappointed. When we fix ourselves in His Living Person and continue following after Him in the journey, we will be changed in the staying. The old will be made new by a divine working.

Another question is in the story of the wedding at Cana. When His mother Mary said, *"They have no wine"* (John 2:3), Jesus responded with a question: *"Woman, what does your concern have to do with Me? My hour has not yet come"* (verse 4). Because of her relationship with Him, Jesus' mother presumed to make Him focus His infinite power upon a very finite purpose. We know from the Gospels that Jesus' miracles happened so that people might know and believe He was Messiah, but He didn't want people to know that yet. This miracle that she's asking for is actually out of place.

Of course it is a beautiful one for us to see, because it makes us think about the marriage supper of the Lamb, where we will be drinking the best wine imaginable—and there won't be a hangover because there won't be a morning after because it will be all one day that goes on and on and on. What a generous God! To think that He would intervene in this very finite moment for the sake of His mother who was concerned that her friends would look bad in town because they ran out of wine. In His generosity, He made them sixty gallons! We have been to Cana, and the place is still a tiny little town. Imagine how sixty gallons of the best wine ever served affected this small group of guests.

This miracle, the first for which Jesus was known, tells us something about God and His miracles. He is willing to give them away to satisfy our immediate needs and desires. How many of those who got drunk on this wine actually ended up in that upper room? How many of them will be at that final wedding feast? The ultimate reason for the miracles of God is to lead people to a revelation of Christ as King and of His Kingdom that is advancing through us and through our prayers. So keep that in mind, even as you make finite requests. God will get glory from every answered prayer.

Lord, give us wisdom that we might number our days and understand how You are working in this hour, that all of our expectation and all of our prayers will be firmly focused on Your will to bring people to Yourself. Don't let us get lost in saying, "God show us Your glory," or in asking for peripheral things that may not necessarily end up bringing people to the wedding feast at the end of the ages, but do use our finite understanding to make requests that bring in your Kingdom.

Everything that God does with us, all of the manifestation of His anointing, the gifts of the Spirit, and so on, are sent so that we might become a circle of influence to bring others to Christ, encouraging them through our example to keep following Him.

It Is Well

Each of us has a divine destiny, but at the center of our obsession must be the One who creates that divine destiny, that One who stood, at the ship's railing in 1873, with the author of the old hymn, "It Is Well with my Soul."

Horatio Spafford had lost all of his children in a shipwreck on that very spot in the Atlantic Ocean. His wife had survived, but his four little daughters had drowned. His son had died from scarlet fever earlier, so now Spafford and his wife Anna, who were friends of D.L. Moody—good people, strong Christians whom you would think God would have protected from harm and sorrow—had lost all of their five children. Instead of lashing back at God, Spafford laid hold of something that is important for us to grasp as well: knowing, doing, and praying the will of God does not mean we have to understand it. We only have to trust the One whose will we seek.

What are you searching for? Let it be Jesus Himself. Anchored to Him, you can go beyond the circumstances of this life. Because of Jesus, you can say with assurance that no matter what may happen in this temporary life, there is a wellness with your soul.

That being said, it is also true that everything is not left to blind trust. We can "hang our hats" on some prayers that are definitely, always in the will of God.

Ancient Pathways

The third verse of the often-quoted 23rd Psalm reads:

He restores my soul;
He leads me in the paths of righteousness
For His name's sake.
(Psalms 23:3)

The psalmist refers to the act of returning to God as the pathway to refreshing. Repentance brings reconciliation with God, and that restoration of fellowship with Him produces revival in our hearts and souls. When we return, we are recreated as God intended in the beginning. Restoration comes as we return to paths of righteousness.

In the psalm, the Hebrew word for path is, *ma'gal*, which means "entrenchment or track" and which comes from a root meaning "to revolve." It gives us a picture of a worn-down path, a visible trench etched into the ground by the frequency of use by those who have gone before. Such "paths of righteousness" are not arbitrary nor are they difficult to discern. We can look at the tread of those who have gone before to see the path our Shepherd intends.

The restoration of our soul is not just a breath of fresh air nor a comforting pause as we go our own way, but a returning to the paths of our Father which have been worn down smooth by many who have walked these paths with Him before us. He has given us a roadmap that keeps us from making one step forward and two steps back. He has set up signposts and guidelines and boundaries that are part of His eternal, unchanging will.

What are some of these signposts? God is recreating a world for His glory. Everything happening today will have its ultimate end in the new Heaven and the new earth. And so our lives and our prayers are connected to God's end-time intentions. We are participating now in the new age to come. There are eternal spiritual elements of His kingdom advancing in us and through us now.

What are some of the ways we can connect our prayers to God's end-time intentions? These are prayers that always reflect the will of God:

Pray His Word. When we pray His Word, we pray the will of the One who committed it to us. This has been a basic practice in prayer from the earliest times. As you read your Bible, take note of particular verses which seem to breathe life into your prayer concerns and pray those words of God as your own words.

We can pray the great prayers of the Bible—found in both the Old and the New Testaments—and we can pray for the desires of God's heart as they appear in Scripture. For example, when we pray for the restoration of natural Israel and the blessing of the Jewish people, we are praying the will of God. (See Psalms 122:6.)

Pray for the Church. When we pray that God's Church (universal and local) would be built up as His residence on earth, we are praying the will of God. To be in the center of God's will, we must find ourselves joyfully and fruitfully planted in the center of His Church.

Pray for the gifts to be restored to the Church. It is God's will that the gifts of the Spirit be restored to the entire Church. It is logical that the five-fold ministry offices given as gifts to the Church are exactly that—five-fold, like the fingers of your hand. An amputation of any one or several of them leaves the body of Christ handicapped in fulfilling its mission, particularly in outreach. If you have teachers you must have pastors; if pastors, then evangelists; if evangelists, then also prophets; and if prophets, then apostles. By the way, in our own opinion, not all who give themselves these designations may be truly so. But that discussion is for another day.

Persistent prayers—and the experiences of the past decades—mean that fewer and fewer serious Bible students deny the existence and historicity of the miraculous in the ongoing expression of the Christian faith. Cessationism is now reaching its own apparent cessation! When we pray, "on earth as it is in Heaven," we are praying for the atmosphere of Heaven where miracles dwell to be made manifest on the earth. It is God's will that we pray for and expect His miracles always!

Pray for believers to obtain their full birthright. The tree of God's will has many branches. I (Mahesh) recall the saying of my native Kenya, *"Binti wa simba na simba"*—"The daughter of a lion is also a lion." It is the will of God that women be given their full birthright as "sons of God." Theirs is not a half-portion. It is God's will that His daughters be restored as equal heirs with His sons. Women receive the same salvation, the same Holy Spirit, the same spiritual gifts, and the same eternal rewards as their brothers. Where the Holy Spirit is fully recognized as the resident Lord of the Church, women are also recognized as full counterparts to men in the faith, in ministry, in the Church.

Simply pray, "Your will be done." When we pray, "Your will be done on earth as it is in Heaven," we are praying the will of God. Watch prayers begin in Heaven, where Jesus is. When we pray, "on earth as it is in Heaven," we begin with the Anointed One. His anointing oil, His manifest presence, flows from the Head down on the rest of His body, the Church.

Rhythms of Grace

Jesus is the Great Amen of all things. And in the end He will come and set the world right. Until then, we advance through watching in prayer. We stretch out our arms as He did on Calvary as we lay down our will and pray for His Kingdom to come. Once we become willing to obey God, His will becomes ours as it was Christ's.

The will of God comes to us as "unforced rhythms of grace."

Jesus resumed talking to the people, but now tenderly. "The Father has given Me all these things to do and say. This is a unique Father-Son operation, coming out of Father and Son intimacies and knowledge. No one knows the Son the way the Father does, nor the Father the way the Son does. But I'm not keeping it to Myself; I'm ready to go over it line by line with anyone willing to listen.

"Are you tired? Worn out? Burned out on religion? Come to me. Get away with Me and you'll recover your life. I'll show you how to take a real rest. Walk with Me and work with Me—watch how I do it. Learn the unforced rhythms of grace. I won't lay anything heavy or ill-fitting on you. Keep company with Me and you'll learn to live freely and lightly" (Matthew 11:27-30 TM).

When Jesus prayed "Your will be done" it was not as if He were boxing the air without a clue as to what God was up to. The Son knew what the Father was doing at all times. It was according to that will that Jesus lived daily in obedience and agreement, thereby aggressively advancing the Kingdom through His life. The miracles He worked were the obvious result of being in agreement with what the Father purposed day-to-day.

Moses and Elijah appeared in visible form before the disciples on the mountain, openly discussing with Jesus the plan of Heaven. (See Matthew 17 and Luke 9.) The heavenly ones affirmed what

Jesus already knew about the Father's mission for Him, and they strengthened Him toward completing that mission, which was to undergo crucifixion. Heaven was watching and listening attentively to bring earth along with it in a strategy for the greatest victory the cosmos could ever embrace. It would be a victory wrought in a manner no human would have conceived. As Moses and Elijah talked with the Christ, the disciples witnessed the spiritual reality that happens when we pray "Your will be done on earth as it is in Heaven." God is ready to effect it through His sons and daughters living on earth if we will but put aside every possibility of our own will and take on His will as our mission.

As we have said, knowing, praying, and doing the will of God are like dancing. He holds us in the embrace of His Spirit and draws us close like a father teaching his daughter how to dance. Dancing is not passive, and neither is prayer. To know His will, we must be familiar with the "dance steps"—His written Word in Scripture. To discern the will of God, we must be familiar with His character personally through an ongoing intimate relationship of faith. To pray the will of God gives us confidence of authority—and answers.

Praying the will of God instigates an *aggressive* advance of the Kingdom of God against the kingdom of darkness. So—pray, and never give up!

ENDNOTES

1. Derek Prince, "The Completeness of the Atonement," *New Wine Magazine*, June 1969.

2. Alister McGrath, *Christianity's Dangerous Idea* (New York: Harper Collins, 2007), book jacket.

CHAPTER 5

As Above, So Below

...On Earth As It Is in Heaven

AGREEING WITH HEAVEN'S PRAYERS.

If you sit on the lakeside, you can see the tree line reflected in a mirror image. Both are realities but one is the substance of the other. What looks like a bridge suspended in midair, appearing to have sky both above and below, makes us think of the relationship between Heaven above and the earth below.

When a watchman prays, "on earth as it is in Heaven," he is praying that the earth will reflect Heaven. To really mean what he prays, he must consider what Heaven is like. In Heaven, there is no night. There is no sickness, sadness, bondage, sin, crying, pain, or death. That's why, when Jesus cast out demons and healed the sick, He said, "The Kingdom of God has come to you." We arise in the same power of the same Spirit to cast out the evil one and to shine Heaven's light into this darkness in which we live. Healing and deliverance attest to the coming of the Kingdom of God.

"Come Holy Spirit. Come and renew the face of the earth!" These words from Psalm 104, frequent in the prayers and homilies of Pope John Paul II, are an apostolic mandate for us as we watch in prayer. The psalm is a prayer that the earth be drenched in the glory and provision of Heaven, and the psalmist's plea opens with the expectant confidence of renewal by the Spirit:

O Lord my God, You are very great:
You are clothed with honor and majesty,

Who cover Yourself with light as with a garment,
Who stretch out the heavens like a curtain.

He lays the beams of His upper chambers in the waters,
Who makes the clouds His chariot,
Who walks on the wings of the wind,

Who makes His angels spirits,
His ministers a flame of fire.

You who laid the foundations of the earth,
So that it should not be moved forever....
The earth is satisfied with the fruit of Your works....

O Lord, how manifold are Your works!
In wisdom You have made them all.
The earth is full of Your possessions....

You hide Your face, they are troubled;
You take away their breath, they die and return to their dust.

You send forth Your Spirit, they are created;
And You renew the face of the earth.
(Psalm 104:1-5,13,24,29-30)

Note the reference to God's angels and ministers. As seen at the throne in John's revelation, the governing body of God's government is a delegation of hosts of men and angels who do his bidding.

Elders, in constant counsel and petition with Him who sits in glory on the great central one, are seated on smaller thrones.

The Church on earth is also the seat of the government of Heaven. We are the mountain of the house of the Lord. Let us allow the Spirit to revise the inner map of our spiritual imaginations, allowing the narratives of Scripture to inspire strategies and motives and direction in an aggressive life of prayer that never fails.

When John saw visions of Heaven, a voice said, "Come up here and I will show you…" (see Rev. 11:12). He saw an open door and as he looked through the door, his eyes were directed to the origin of all that is good. It was a throne and One seated upon it.

The open door through which John approached the throne reminds us of the words of Jesus often used as a parable for our initial salvation: *"Behold I stand at the door and knock. If anyone hears My voice and opens the door, I will come in to him and dine with him, and he with Me"* (Rev. 3:20). As we open our hearts to the mind of the Spirit, He draws our attention to the throne. As we gaze upon it our understanding changes and the language of our prayers changes. Now instead of praying from beneath a brass Heaven, we pray from the reality that we are seated in heavenly places. Notice Jesus' words to those whose eyes had been healed to see: *"To him who overcomes I will grant to sit with Me on My throne…"* (Rev. 3:21). While the door of our hearts opened to Him when we first believed, too often we never step through that door in our prayers. We think from earth to Heaven rather than believe from Heaven to earth. The Lamb is the One who brings us to the throne. From there, we loose prayers that the earth and its inhabitants will be recreated in the image of Him who made them.

This great division between Heaven and earth opened once for all when the Lamb's blood was poured out and the veil was rent. He has brought us near. In the throne and surrounding it are all the dimensions of declarations and proclamations, things that have been established: every human need met, all evil conquered, every provision made, all hope renewed. His throne is established in righteousness. His throne is established in justice. It was settled at the Cross.

Praying from Heaven to earth is not some fantastic voyage of our own creation. Prayer is not reserved for mystics. Open your heart, open your Bible, open your mind, open your mouth and pray!

It's About His Throne

The overarching theme of the Book of Revelation is a *throne*, a throne that you and I have a personal relationship with. John's revelation is about government. It is about the unveiling of the government that rules the whole world.

When we stand before the heavenly throne in prayer, we serve as reflectors—reflecting the image of the Savior to our world.

Revelation 1:4 says, *"Grace to you and peace from Him who is and who was and who is to come."* This is a message of grace and peace to you from the throne from Jesus Christ. We need to receive it. We need to go through the open door in order to enter the throne room.

"After these things I looked, and behold, a door standing open in heaven" (Rev. 4:1). Doors, you know, are wonderful things unless you want to get in and the door is closed, or worse yet, locked, or if there's a doorkeeper who won't let you in. But what we see here is that this door to heaven is standing open. This Lord tells John, *"I have set before you an open door, and no one can shut it;..."* (Rev. 3:8).

"Around the throne were twenty-four thrones, and on the thrones I [John] saw twenty-four elders sitting, clothed in white robes; and they had crowns of gold on their heads" (Rev. 4:4). A crown would indicate they must be ruling something, wouldn't it?

Who are these elders? We don't know. But we do know that the seat of all government is surrounded by other seats of government where elders sit. As we look at this scene, we suddenly realize that this government works by delegating its authority. What are those elders there for? They are there to rule. So they are taking authority from the throne to be handed out.

The nature of this government is reflected in what we see around it: We see covenant promise depicted in the emerald rainbow surrounding the throne. This rainbow is God's promise of peace and rest and blessing; we see life, creatures of all kinds, 24 elders, all created things. The message? This government rules through life and is all about life.

In Revelation 1:18, the One who stands in the midst of the throne says, *"I am He who lives, and was dead, and behold, I am alive forevermore."* Then John looked, *"and I heard the voice of many angels around the throne, the living creatures, and the elders; and the number of them was ten thousand times ten thousand, and thousands of thousands,"* (Rev. 5:11). This throne is really about life.

It's About His Light

Look back at Revelation chapter 1, and let's look at another couple of aspects of this government. In this introduction to the vision, we see all kinds of light sources. (See Revelation 1:12-16.)

*I saw **seven golden lampstands**, and in the midst of the **seven lampstands** One like the Son of Man, clothed with a garment down to the feet and girded about the chest with a **golden band**. His head and hair were white like wool, as white as snow, and His eyes like a **flame of fire**; His feet were like fine brass, as if refined in a furnace, and His voice as the sound of many waters; He had in His right hand **seven stars**, out of His mouth went a sharp two-edged* *sword, and His countenance was like the **sun shining** in its strength.* (Rev. 1:12-16, emphasis added).

This government is about both life and light.

It's About His Righteousness

The One who is described here is glorious: His hair, His hands, His feet, His eyes. When we see Him we realize we have been created like Him! He has a very unusual tongue, a tongue like a sword with two edges. It cuts both ways. He is truth. This government is about life and light and truth.

Romans 14:17 describes this government, "The Kingdom of God is not a matter of eating and drinking, but of righteousness…" (NIV). That is moral righteousness, thinking and acting the right way. There *is* a right way. There *is* a right and wrong.

This throne rules through truth and judgment, also called justice. We don't like to talk too much about judgment. Usually when judgment comes up people get nervous and start accusing you of being legalistic or religious. They don't want to talk about the possibility of judgment. But this book at the end of our Bibles, this revelation given to John, is all about the seat of government and judgment. There are seals and trumpets and angels and all kinds of layers of judgment that are unfolding.

But let us remember who opens and unfolds them: The One like the Son of Man, the One who clothed Himself in the weakness of human flesh, the One in whom we have a covenant, an everlasting covenant.

It's About Peace and Joy

As we keep reading in the book of Revelation, we see the circle moving out farther and farther from the seat of all government and the throne of authority, and as we see it moving out, there is this great panorama of light and life and power, and there is singing. Singing! Where does singing come from? Happy people! This book is filled with singing and every time a judgment comes, this great throng of light and life all around the throne sing and worship. Righteousness, Peace and Joy! Singing. This government is about joy. It's about good news. It's about victory and triumph. It is about justice for all the oppressed. It is about relief that comes at last to the whole world and to the nations of the whole world.

It's about peace like a sea of glass (see Rev. 4:6). Perfect peace. Every wave stilled, every wind, every storm calmed—and not because the throne is sleeping. There are lightnings and thunders coming out of the throne. Life is bursting out from the One on the throne to many who have been brought near the throne. That life is so full of love that it causes that great sea of multitudes of people from every tribe, nation, language, and tongue to be perfectly calm in the presence of the power that's coming from the throne.

FROM THE THRONE

Remember, this throne works through delegation. We see this multitude of people from every nation coming up to this throne. Their voices are listened to by the One who sits on the throne. The events on the earth unfold the authority of that throne through the prayers of the saints.

We've been brought near to this throne. We have been brought near through the blood of the Lamb. We share in this Kingdom of righteousness, peace, and joy. And so in the face of difficulties, whether they be economic challenges, personal issues such as sickness, relationship problems, a child in trouble or an elderly parent, we can obtain a word of authority from the righteous seat of government. We can draw near to that throne of grace through the blood that has been shed for us. We draw near through the prayer of faith and find real help for every need.

Jesus' poignant words to His disciples in the Garden of Gethsemane were, *"Could you not watch with Me one hour?"* (Matt. 26:40). We all hear these words to this day. They come to us as Jesus searches under the olive trees by moonlight. It is midnight. He is looking for His friends. Searching to find them, hoping they are awake and that this time they will not fail Him.

Through the Lord Jesus, we step in by faith to that place of authority that He has given us through His blood, a place before His throne. It is a place of perfect peace in the face of every storm of this earth. There we see His light. The scepter of oppression and darkness and bondage and judgment and fear is lifted off. Now the gifts of healing, miracles, and faith can flow. The prayers of the saints work with the angels, the elders, and the four living creatures.

Angels Watching With Us

We traveled to England, to Coventry, to celebrate Canon Andrew White's birthday. Canon Andrew is a good friend and was the youngest Canon in the history of Coventry Cathedral. As he was giving us a quick walking tour of the cathedral, we came into a chapel that is dedicated to Christ in Gethsemane. All of the stained glass, the sculpture, and symbolic things that are in there have to do with the night in Gethsemane as Jesus looked toward the Cross. As we walked in, Andrew said, "This is Christ in Gethsemane Chapel, and that's the angel of the watch," and he pointed to a piece of artwork that has been on the chapel wall since they built the chapel. The artist's rendition of this particular angel struck me (Bonnie), because it looked like one I had seen before.

In the spring of 1994, I woke up one night to see an angel standing at the foot of my bed. It was a very specific angel. This was not an angel dressed in white or filled with white light. He had a dark body, dark wings, and he was all black, except that the surface of his body shimmered with liquid gold that moved as if it were alive. I would come to realize the significance of this angel's dark visage as being a messenger of God and His glory even during the darkest hours. Such was the nature of his coloring—as the night—but flashing with living Shekinah. I also knew that it was when things might seem the most obscure, dark, or most desperate that we must know and believe that God who watches over us neither slumbers nor sleeps. And just as He often brought the greatest deliverances in the darkest times of old, He still works His wonders to the amazement of man today. I sat up out of my sleep and there was this figure. My mind was telling me, "If it's dark, that should be bad," but I knew he was good and very, very powerful. From his countenance, I also had this knowledge that this angel was now going to be with us, so to speak. I had never figured out what this angel was, even though Mahesh and others had offered suggestions. None of it had ever really hit home.

I didn't really focus on it, but every once in awhile I would think again about the way that angel had come. The Bible says that angels are God's ministers, sent forth to the heirs of salvation, and so I knew they bring us all kinds of helpful things, whether or not we are aware of the specific purposes of God in that moment.

Well, when Canon Andrew pointed and said, "This is the watch angel," I looked up. It was the angel that I had seen in 1994! The artist depicted the watch angel with Jesus in Gethsemane, helping Him through as He kept the watch at that particular time of trial.

The whole experience really charged me up again about the preciousness of The Watch to the Lord and to our generation as we look forward to the coming of the Lord. It connected for me the idea that the earth in a sense is going to be entering into her Gethsemane with its particular kind of trial and testing, and it brought me home with an additional sense of commissioning. I could see how God had brought us together in Charlotte, North

Carolina from the ends of the earth, from different circumstances, through many trials, through many joys, and had forged something, a fellowship of watchmen, of people who have, as a focal point of their spiritual activity this prayer meeting called The Watch. I knew that the Lord is with us, but I now began to believe that He had sent out His special messengers, including the angel of The Watch, possibly even the one that was with Jesus.

I am just as certain that the messengers of the Lord are standing ready, His ministers whom He makes flames of fire, sent out to those who are heirs of salvation, like the angels who came to Daniel on behalf of a nation, and like those who came down to bring Lot out before they destroyed Sodom and Gomorrah, and like the one who visited Gideon as he was threshing out wheat in a wine press one midnight.

Angels on Assignment

I (Mahesh) remember when I came to the United States many years ago. I had never been outside of Kenya. I went to New York and I had to catch a flight to Dallas. I had never seen airplanes this big. I had never seen a giant airport.

When I went to check in, they asked, "What happened to your other ticket? You have no ticket." I was barely eighteen, and I had only five dollars in my pocket. I didn't know anybody in New York.

Suddenly this giant of a man came along. He was wearing a big cowboy hat, huge Texas boots, and a big smile. He slapped me on the back and said, "Hey, boy. You look like you're in trouble." I told him what they had just told me, that I didn't have a ticket. He said, "Wait here." He went up to the counter and came back and said, "You are sitting by my side."

I said, "To where?"

He said, "To Dallas." That's exactly where I needed to go.

We flew to Dallas, sitting side-by-side, and every now and then I would take another look at him. He really was the biggest man I had ever seen, and his cowboy hat was enormous. The plane landed in Dallas and they pushed steps up to the exit door. My friends were waiting there to receive me. My friends had visited Kenya and I wanted to introduce my giant friend to them.

I turned around and there was nobody. Suddenly I realized: *that was an angel that God sent!*

It's good to know that God can take care of us that way. Just as there are angels helping individuals, so do nations have angels assigned to them to fight for God's righteous cause. Many nations are the focus of a wrestling match between light and darkness. God is awakening Christians as watchmen for their nations, deploying us in prayer, fasting and proclaiming the Gospel. God has predetermined the boundaries of the nations and those who dwell in them that we might seek and find the Lord (see Acts 17:26). As active citizens we must pray and fast for our nations as part of our personal spiritual call to faithfulness.

What happens in the politics of your nation affects and is affected by you. Part of your spiritual calling is to exercise authority as an ambassador of Heaven within the boundaries of your national citizenship. Pray that good men and women will rule in your nation so that holy angels will have access to and influence in your land.

As it was in the days of Daniel, angels are all around us. Many are waiting for our prayers to loose them according to the will of God. We can invite their ministry now as we head into end-time storms. God-of-the-Angel-Armies is our refuge and ark of safety. His hosts are waiting to do His will.

While we welcome the assistance that angels bring from heaven's throne, too much obsession with angelic beings can be problematic. Angels never call attention to themselves. They accomplish their mission, but they always point back to Jesus. The

Bible warns that in the last days antichrists will come. *Antichrist* means "opposed or in place of" Christ. Anytime a person starts relying on supernatural beings other than Jesus for counsel and revelation, they are in danger of coming under the influence of a false spirit.

THE MOUNTAIN OF THE LORD

Is the Church only a refuge that we run into? This idea needs to change. The Church is, in fact, the place from which God sends us out to conquer. We believe that God's word for the Church today is to take back the territory that has been lost. For generations God's people have been giving up to the enemy our authority to shape and influence culture.

Over 300 years ago, Yale and Harvard were founded as institutions of higher learning to educate ministers of the Gospel. Now these same institutions aggressively promote atheism and socialism and are extremely critical of Christian thinking. A great champion of conservative values, the late William F. Buckley, was prohibited from delivering his commencement speech at Yale because of its overtly Christian content. He decided to expand his speech into a book, *God and Man at Yale*, in which he exposed the aggressive liberal agenda of his alma mater and rallied a movement around him to restore the Judeo-Christian foundations of our nation and culture beginning with public education.

If we leave a vacuum in any area of our society, something will fill it. It is time for new voices to arise and take back the territory that has been lost, and it is the charge of the Church to lead the way.

The Bible tells us that in the last days the mountain of the Lord's temple will be established as chief among the mountains; it will be raised above the hills, and all nations will stream to it (see Isa. 2:2).

Many people shall come and say, "Come, and let us go up to the mountain of the Lord, to the house of the God of Jacob; He will teach us His ways, and we shall walk in His paths." For out of Zion shall go forth the law, and the word of the Lord from Jerusalem (Isaiah 2:3).

We believe this mountain is the end-time Church in her glory. We are living in the last days, and we are on a journey to ruling and reigning from the top of this mountain. We need to move away from the idea of the Church as only a refuge or a hospital. While this is true and the healing and safety we need are found there, the Church is ordained as the place from which God sends us out to extend His Kingdom. The Cross of Christ has planted us at the top of the chief of the mountains where He has conquered every power and principality, even death. Jesus said, "If I be lifted up, I will draw all men unto Me" (see John 12:32). Isaiah 2:3 says, *"all nations will stream to it"* (NIV). The mandate of the Church is a missionary mandate that extends not only to individuals, but to the high places in every sphere and every level of every nation. The Church is the agent of change, not only to bring people into the Kingdom, but also to bring the Kingdom into the earth. The history of the Church is a history of influence that shaped culture.

In Numbers 27:12, God tells Moses, *"Go up this mountain in the Abarim range and see the land I have given the Israelites"* (NIV). It is the same vantage point from which we will prevail. Too often we allow our perspective to be defined by the other powers and high places in our society. The voices of our media, entertainment, government, and our educational system have all shaped our culture with the message that the Church is irrelevant, repressive, and powerless. But we see from Isaiah that the Church is not just one voice, nor one hill among many. The Church is the chief of mountains and exercises authority and influence over every other hill! In order to fulfill our mandate, we need to experience a paradigm shift in our understanding. We are seated in heavenly places. It is from this vantage on the chief among mountains that we engage in spiritual warfare, intercession, and go out to take back our culture and society.

We are in a season of restoration as individuals, as the Church and as a nation. Wherever you are and whatever challenges you face, you are defined by the mountain of the Lord.

We read in Exodus 15:17-18, singing of the Lord and concerning His covenant people,

You will bring them in and plant them
In the mountain of Your inheritance,
In the place, O Lord, which You have made
For Your own dwelling,
The sanctuary, O Lord, which Your hands have established.
The Lord shall reign forever and ever.

So we're not just individuals, doing our own things, running to other mountains for our identity. We're not hiding in a cave. But where God is giving us grace to find ourselves as one, we are putting our shields together. Each of us has strength in one area or another. Some are good in marketing. Some are good in computers. Some are good in the medical field. So, from the chief of the mountains we do spiritual warfare, we do intercession, and we influence each of the other mountains.

The vision for overcoming and vision for taking the land for God's covenant people—where does it come from? It comes from the perspective gained on top of the mountain of the Lord. Don't you have to get in an elevated place in order to get a real perspective? If you are down on the same level, then all you can see is what is immediately around you. You might have people coming to you and telling you what's in the next neighborhood, but if you go to the mountaintop, you can see the lay of the land. You can see the rivers; you can see where there are strongholds. You can see all of those things, and you can compare notes with others on the mountain of the local church, so it is not just an individual revelation. And it's certainly not defined by the loudest and shrillest voices of the mass media.

The media will try to define us. That should never be acceptable. "This is the Church," they say. No, they cannot define our values. We define what we see from the mountain, and we define *their* values. They cannot tell us, "Oh don't call this a baby. Call it a fetus." If we change the language and call it a fetus instead of a baby, then we can kill it without moral consequence. We must not allow the spirit of humanism to change the definitions in our language. It's that basic.

One morning the Lord spoke to me (Bonnie) and said, "Bonnie, if you only look for Me in the crowd you will never find Me." It was a very clear word. Obviously, He was speaking about the tendency of individuals to assume that if a multitude is saying something, then it must be right, regardless of the motivation behind it.

We are in a great strategic battle; watchmen occupy a key position. That is why God says, "We are seated in heavenly places." The Church has the authority, especially in the last days.

We have authority today to say to certain demonic agencies, "You cannot come any further. And we as a Church can say, "Cancer, stand still and come out." We can say to curses, to things that would rob us of our inheritance, rob us of our finances, rob us of our children, "Stop," just as Joshua said, "Stop" to the sun (see Josh. 10:12). We say, "Stop to any and every curse trying to take your blessing away."

We don't blame past things. We don't blame others. We just take our place of authority and power. Any kind of curse coming against you or your family, whether it is a poverty curse, or infirmity or any other curse, we are as the mountain of the house of the

Lord, joining together and saying, "Stop in Jesus' name," and the deliverance comes.

The Church (*ekklesia*) of Jesus on earth as it is in Heaven is a great legislative body. Man, living creatures, and angels all take their places separated out from the kingdom of darkness as servants of Him who has begun to reign. For the generations who yet have a role of destiny to fulfill upon the old earth, we have seen the importance of moving from within ourselves and the strain and demands of private ambition, to become that kingdom of priests who serve at His behest. In Heaven, the prayers of the royal priesthood are a causative factor in the timing of events that bring justice to a world whose inhabitants have been held hostage to satan and his wiles.

"On Earth As It Is in Heaven"

Commenting on Jesus' approach to power and authority wielded through His particular style of praying, Ferdinand Hahn, a German professor of New Testament, wrote:

> Attention must be given not only to the content but also to the outward form of the Lord's Prayer in its original version: it is not a prayer in Hebrew but in the Aramaic vernacular—not totally out of the question in contemporary Judaism, but unusual. This means again that Jesus removes prayer from the liturgical sphere of sacral language and places it right in the midst of everyday life…here is no longer any distinction in principle between assembly for worship and the service of Christians in the world…. For the Christian community worship does not take place in a separate realm but in the midst of the existing world; it therefore includes service by the faithful in everyday life.[1]

We must step up to the plate. Our assemblies of prayer are meant to enter the world and intervene that Heaven has its way below. Prayer is an eternal force in the sense that it enters beyond time and space to where no time is, before the throne of God. There prayer lays hold of the eternal counsel and utters its "Amen!" back to time and space. This is the eternal nature of prayer. The Bible says that Jesus ever lives to make intercession for us. And so, entering into intercession specifically is really just coming in line with the harmony of Heaven, personally connecting up with what Jesus is already doing. His intercession is an intervention by His blood. As the Church is awakened to watching and praying, specifically to praying intercession, we enter into that place of harmony with Jesus' ministry in Heaven and we reflect it as mirrors reflect the sun, bringing Heaven down to earth to intervene.

ENDNOTE

1. Ferdinand Hahn, *The Worship of the Early Church* (Philadelphia: Fortress Press, 1973), 22, 38, 106.

CHAPTER 6

Alive With Three Square Meals

Give Us This Day
Our Daily Bread...

OBTAINING THE PROVISION OF THE CROSS—
PRIESTLY IDENTITY, PRIESTLY PROVISION.

"You don't really have to eat do you?" he asked....

"We don't have to do anything," Papa stated rather strongly.

"Then why do You eat?" Mack inquired.

"To be with you, honey."[1]

In the book, *The Shack*, the main character Mack Phillips often shares meals with "Papa," God the Father, meals that Papa prepared for Mack. In this scene, Mack realizes that what Papa is doing for him is purely out of Papa's desire to have fellowship with him; the only opportunity is in meeting Mack at the point of his need.

Our heavenly Father knows what we need before we ask Him and He meets us more than halfway, but He enjoys it when we give something back to Him. Think about the people you most enjoy hanging out with, the people who most energize and delight you. They are not the people who talk only about themselves and their own needs. The people you most enjoy being with are those who bring something to the table and don't just take away. In His prayers, Jesus mentioned Heaven twice as much as earth. He wasn't praying pie-in-the-sky and He wasn't praying "I need pie." He had come from Heaven and knew He was returning there so He was praying both the beginning and end into the middle of the story. He knew what He was talking about when He told His disciples, "Seek first the kingdom of heaven and all these things will be added to you" (see Matt. 6:33).

Jesus was saying that once people reorient themselves to live from the end of the story forward, they will realize that their ticket to the destination is all-inclusive. They can begin to lend the resource they possess, hearts, minds, and bodies, to the cause. The devil's strategy is to keep us from ever moving our prayer beyond "us four and no more."

Let's get beyond that. Let's break the cycle of circular praying that begins and ends with "me," and seek the true Bread of Heaven, Jesus Himself.

THE SHEPHERD WHO IS BREAD

In *The Message*, Eugene Peterson's paraphrase of the Bible, Psalm 23 comes out like this:

> *God, my shepherd! I don't need a thing. You have bedded me down in lush meadows, You find me quiet pools to drink from. True to Your word,*

> *You let me catch my breath and send me in the right direction. Even when the way goes through*

> *Death Valley, I'm not afraid when You walk at my side. Your trusty shepherd's crook makes me feel secure. You*

serve me a six-course dinner right in front of my enemies. You revive my drooping head; my cup brims with blessing (Psalms 23:1-5 TM).

The "shepherd" of Psalm 23 is a verb, denoting the action of feeding. This shepherd, "prepares a table before me" (verse 5). After we have been fed, Jesus says to us, "If you love Me, feed My sheep" (see John 21:17).

He is taking it to a whole new level, praying that God would enable us to fulfill our priestly ministry before the world. We can turn and feed others because of Jesus' rich presence in our lives. The Bread for our lives, like the Israelites' manna or the Old Testament priests' ever-fresh bread in the tabernacle, is actually the presence of Christ that feeds us and strengthens us for the work of giving witness to Him through everything we do and say all day long.

"Our fathers ate the manna in the desert; as it is written, 'He gave them bread from heaven to eat.'"

Then Jesus said to them, "Most assuredly, I say to you, Moses did not give you the bread from heaven, but My Father gives you the true bread from heaven. For the bread of God is He who comes down from heaven and gives life to the world."

Then they said to Him, "Lord, give us this bread always."

And Jesus said to them, "I am the bread of life. He who comes to Me shall never hunger, and he who believes in Me shall never thirst....For I have come down from heaven, not to do My own will, but the will of Him who sent Me. (John 6:31-35,38)

[The children of Israel] *all ate the same spiritual food, and all drank the same spiritual drink. For they drank of that spiritual Rock that followed them, and that Rock was Christ* (1 Corinthians 10:3-4).

Earlier in John 6 we see the event in Jesus' earthly ministry that caused Him to say, "I am the bread of life." The disciples needed to find bread for the large crowd had followed Jesus into the wilderness. They didn't have the money to buy enough bread to feed that crowd. There were three things that Jesus asked the disciples to do so they could participate in this miracle. None of them were supernatural. (1) Have the people sit down (verse 10); (2) distribute the food Jesus gave them (verse 11); and (3) gather up the leftovers (verse 12). Jesus' part in the multiplication of the loaves and the fishes was to perform the miracle. The disciples' part was to do what He told them to do.

God delights to partner with His priesthood—that's you and me! Perhaps we approach the ministry given us as His witnesses in the way the disciples did at first. On the basis of our ability, it's impossible to produce, perform, or create a miracle. But that is not our part in the miracles that God does. When we do our part, which is to go where Jesus goes, listen for His instruction, and serve and obey, nothing is impossible.

His presence is not just for our own "consumption." We eat to be filled with Him so that we might be multiplied out as food, through Christ, to the world. The miracle of the multiplication of the loaves and fishes was a parable of our lives. When the disciples each gathered an entire basket filled with leftover fragments of Christ's miracle, it was a sign for each man personally that as he participated with Christ in the will of God, he would see God's miracles, provide food for those who are hungry, and carry away the spoils. Each disciple was meant to become a basketful of blessing for others.

So when we pray, "Give us this day our daily bread," it is not just a prayer that God would provide physical food, the clothing, the house payment etc.; it is a prayer for the presence of Christ to dwell in us richly, feeding us and making us food for others who do not know Him.

43,000-Ton God

The Lord is our Shepherd and He provides all kinds of "bread" for us—especially as we apply for His provision in prayer—so that we can feed others in turn.

In Chapter 5, we mentioned Canon Andrew White, who in recent days spends his time in Baghdad, Iraq, where he is vicar of St. George's Church, perhaps the most dangerous pastorate on earth at this time. Our church supports Andrew financially and at every watch, praying with fasting.

One of Andrew's primary ministries is feeding numbers of widows and orphans. During a recent Christmas season, relief agencies had sent plenty of pasta and rice, but no meat. We were watching and praying for Andrew's needs through Friday night, and then that Sunday Andrew prayed, "Lord, our orphans and widows here in Baghdad have no meat. Help us Lord."

The next day, he was having breakfast in a hotel, wearing his clerical collar, and a tall man walked up to him and asked, "How's it going, Reverend?"

"Things are OK," Andrew said.

The tall man said, "Are you helping the people?"

"We are trying to."

The man came closer, and Andrew noted that he was very tall. The big man asked, "By the way, can you use some meat?"

Andrew replied, "Can we use some meat? Yes, we can!"

The man said, "All right. I've got some meat for you."

"How much?"

"I can supply you with 43,000 tons of meat."

Andrew's hope when he prayed was for a few pounds of meat. God gave him 43,000 *tons*. He also supplied big refrigerated trucks, with drivers, so that the meat could be distributed across Baghdad and other regions in Iraq.

Andrew marveled, "I prayed Sunday night. Monday morning there's this tall man. Was this an angel?"

Whether or not it was an angel, it was a prophetic signal to God's believing people. God wants to supply all of our needs from the wealth of His supply:

God can pour on the blessings in astonishing ways so that you're ready for anything and everything, more than just ready to do what needs to be done. As one psalmist puts it,

> *He throws caution to the winds,*
> *giving to the needy in reckless abandon.*
> *His right-living, right-giving ways*
> *never run out, never wear out.*

> *This most generous God who gives seed to the farmer that becomes bread for your meals is more than extravagant with you. He gives you something you can then give away, which grows into full-formed lives, robust in God, wealthy in every way, so that you can be generous in every way, producing with us great praise to God* (2 Corinthians 9:8-11 TM).

As we learn to watch and pray God wants to give us 43,000-ton breakthroughs. During our years of watching and praying, we have continued to see that God always adds something extra. It's like when you eat in New Orleans, where you'll often get *lagniappe*—a Cajun custom of hospitality. You may order blackened red fish, but on the side they will bring you a steaming bowl of Cajun shrimp. One time I (Mahesh) pointed out that I didn't order the shrimp and they said, "It's just something extra. " I don't know if God is Cajun, but He has lots of lagniappe for us. He throws in extras in answer to prayer.

In Jesus' simple one-liner, "give us this day our daily bread," He acknowledged that we believers, as the priests of God, are utterly dependent on Him today for the bread of provision as were the Levites of old, who ate from the temple offerings. Here are some first-hand testimonies of His provision from our own watchers in Charlotte. You can see how every time, God not only provided generously, but He made it possible for people to provide for others.

Financial provision. I had begun to face some financial struggles due, in part, to the rising price of gas. When Commitment Sunday (for the church building campaign) rolled around, I prayed to the Lord for guidance. I felt led to give what I could—even though normally I would have been able to give more. As I sowed my first-fruit offering, I prayed that the Lord would begin to supply me with more funds so I could give more and still pay my bills.

God gave me quite a testimony in the week that followed! In her safety deposit box, my mom found some savings bonds that were in my name from when I was a baby. When I cashed them, my account doubled! I then proceeded to receive a refund for something that I never thought could be refunded—what favor! Between the Sunday that I gave my first-fruits offering and the Friday of that week, my bank account *tripled*!

Stolen goods restored—with interest. At Christmastime, my home was burglarized. My new television, laptop, and iPod were taken. Realistically, I didn't expect to see that stuff again. Several weeks later, the detective called to tell me, "We're still looking," but I could tell from his message that I shouldn't hold my breath. Nothing had been recovered so far.

In the meantime, I was praying for the thief or thieves, asking that the conviction of the Holy Spirit would come upon them and that they would return what was stolen. A few more weeks passed as I continued to pray the same prayer.

Then on a Sunday evening my phone rang. The caller ID told me that it was a pay phone. I normally would not answer, but that time, I felt that I should. I didn't recognize the voice on the other end of the phone, but the young man on the line asked, "Is this Bill?"

I said, "Yes."

He then said, "You are a Christian, right?"

I said, "As a matter of fact, I am."

Then he said, "This is going to sound weird, but I have your laptop computer." He told me he had just moved from another city three weeks ago, and when he had arrived, he was approached with what he thought was a legitimate offer of a computer for $300. He bought the computer, but later found a file folder buried deep in the computer that had for whatever reason not been erased by the thieves. Strangely enough, the only information stored in the file were some dreams that I had written down and my contact information. The young man had read the dreams and determined that I must be a Christian. He had recently become hungry for the Lord and knew the Holy Spirit was convicting him to turn the computer to its owner in order to restore his fellowship with God. I agreed to meet with him at a local fast food restaurant so he could return my computer.

On the way to the restaurant, I felt the Lord prompting me to go to the ATM and take out three hundred dollars in cash, the price the young man had paid for my stolen computer. When I met with him, I found out that he was prepared to go to jail in order to obey the Lord. Instead, he met his first Spirit-filled friend. He was astonished when I ended our meeting by giving him the three hundred dollars that the Lord had asked me to bring. He was hungry for the Lord and looking for a church family. The Lord heard both of our prayers.

Bread for the children. We have seen many dramatic miracles in the context of watching and praying together for our children. One mother in our congregation recently told us, "I know that it is the anointing and prayers of The Watch that have made the difference in my son's life. Before we moved here, he did not progress at all, and now his doctors are amazed."

When she first arrived three years earlier, her son had been diagnosed as developmentally delayed. He could not walk, chew food, or communicate. The prognosis given by doctors and therapists was not positive. However, recently her son's doctors, therapists, and special needs teachers reported in their assessments that he has progressed the most of any child they have worked with. This all began when she joined herself to a church family that watches and prays together on a regular basis.

Another mother, desperate for a miracle for her son, heard the testimony of the healings that take place in The Watch in our local church body. She booked a flight from their home in Montana to Charlotte, North Carolina to bring her terminally ill son for just one night in the corporate watch. We received a letter a few weeks later reporting that when they went to the doctor following The Watch, he couldn't believe the transformation in her son's health.

Many of our young people join us in The Watch every week. One of our young watchmen had struggled in school over the years, but when he reached middle school, he was unable to keep up with the demands of his grade level and was failing all of his classes. He went through a battery of tests and assessments, but the experts were baffled by the results. They said they were sorry, but this young man was not suited for higher education and they suggested that he be placed in a less challenging environment.

When he received that report from his parents, the young man said, "Mom—they don't know. They don't have the last word." He kept coming to The Watch and we kept praying for him. He chose not to believe the report of the specialists, but he kept pressing on toward his goal of graduating from high school and attending a university.

When this young man graduated with a high grade point average and got accepted at a university, the tutors and specialists who had worked with him over the years told his parents that never in their careers had they seen a student with such low assessment scores do so well academically.

After more than 14 years of keeping The Watch as a church family, we have a new generation of our children raised under the glory cloud of The Watch who are becoming priestly bread for the world. They are moving into positions of influence that range from cultural to business to legal to political. These "children of The Watch" are arising to shine as lights for the next generation. We see that watching in prayer is a lifestyle, and so do they. Through patience, perseverance, faithfulness, and joy, The Watch is bearing rich fruit in the next generation.

NOT BY BREAD ALONE

Every person must eat to live. The Bible is filled with the themes of eating—eating to sustain life, to keep covenant, and in connection with celebration.

We see Jesus tested in the wilderness during which time He ate nothing. When He was hungry, satan spoke to Him. "If you are the Son of God, command this stone to become bread." Jesus' reply was from the words of Moses spoken to Israel as a warning against temptation once they had entered the blessing promised them through God's covenant:

He humbled you, allowed you to hunger, and fed you with manna which you did not know nor did your fathers know, that He might make you know that man shall not live by bread alone; but man lives by every word that proceeds from the mouth of the Lord (Deuteronomy 8:3).

In another place, Jesus said, *"My food is to do the will of Him who sent Me, and to finish His work"* (John 4:34). The bread upon which Jesus fed, even as He was physically hungry from fasting, was obedience to the Father's pleasure.

This is His priestly identity, and we share in it. So when we pray, "Give us this day our daily bread," we are praying that the Bread of Heaven (Jesus' Spirit) will be fresh in us every day and that His presence will be an aroma of life wherever we go.

For several years as a young Christian, whenever I (Bonnie) heard anointed preaching, I would have a physical sense of being filled with fresh baked bread. I could even smell it. When I was a child, my mother baked homemade bread weekly. For one day a week, the house was always filled with that aroma. All who entered would feel a sense of well-being, provision, security, of coming home. My parents and brothers and I would often stand at the kitchen sideboard sharing the hot bread dripping with butter and honey.

When we began The Watch in Charlotte, the aroma of fresh baked bread and a sensation of being filled with it occurred frequently. It was a prophetic message to us: Jesus Christ is the Bread of Heaven. He comes to us fresh day by day and He is a more tangible sustenance than even the manna that was given Israel in the desert. As we are awakened to His presence, He will feed us as His children and as His priests.

ENDNOTE

1. William P. Young, *The Shack* (Los Angeles: Windblown Media, 2007), 199.

CHAPTER 7

Forgiven and Forgiving

Forgive Our Debts As We Forgive Our Debtors...

LIVING IN THE POWER OF THE CROSS.

A few years ago, I (Bonnie) awoke from a terrible nightmare. I had dreamed that a malevolent intruder had entered my father's home in the darkness. I was trying to warn my father and stop the thief, but I was unable to do so before a bright flash of gunfire jolted me out of sleep. I rebuked the nightmare, and I bound the devil. Then I had that dream two more times exactly as I dreamed it at first.

I called my father and I talked to him. He was running an old trading post out in the desert of the Wild West. In talking to him I discovered that in fact he was giving refuge to a woman and her two children whose common-law husband and the father of the children was an abuser, a violent and dangerous man. They'd done what they could do with the law, obtaining restraining orders and such, but there were no police stations out there. So, old sheriff that he was, he just strapped his .44 on his side and said, "I'm ready. I'm not afraid."

Justice should prevail. What do you do when your nightmare becomes reality? What do you do when the worst thing imaginable happens? How do you respond? Who do you turn to? Who do you blame? Where do you go for justice? How do you undo what's been done?

When I received the call that my father had been found dead, I remember having the sense that the Lord was standing there with his arms outstretched in both directions as they had been on the Cross. I knew that how I responded to this event was going to affect the rest of my life.

I flew west immediately, and I was there in my father's home within 24 hours of when he had been slain. The house's emptiness was palpable. I wanted to reach back through it and lay hold of him in his vibrant life and bring him safely into that empty room where I stood.

I caught sight of a small rug that he had used as a cover on his coffee table. It was lying on the carpet off to one side of the room. I was about to pick it up and replace it when something stopped me. Instead I just lifted the edge of it with my toe. And there in the carpet was the last physical element of the life of my father— his blood pooled on the carpet. Trembling with tears, I stooped down and touched the edge of the bloodstain. My heart seemed to stop. My thoughts were suspended between fear and despair, between faith and disbelief, between shock and revenge. It seemed as if all of the sound in the whole of creation had gone silent.

My father had just passed his 60th birthday. We were looking forward to having my children, his grandchildren, and him enjoy one another. He was one of the last of the old-time American cowboys and so with him part of our national heritage had died, and his grandchildren had not yet gotten to experience and know their heritage.

As my trembling hand rested on the crusted, dark spot, somewhere from deep within a cry of my own anguish began to rise and as it rose, another voice spoke louder in my ear. This was no voice of humans or demons. It sounded like my father's voice within my Heavenly Father's voice. Speaking out of the blood at my fingertips, he said, "Take no vengeance."

"FATHER, FORGIVE THEM"

Hanging on the Cross with His blood everywhere, Jesus said, *"Father, forgive them, for they do not know what they do"* (Luke 23:34). This word of love, this prayer, was unexpected and undeserved.

It revealed the purpose for which He would hang there for the next six hours until His death—that in spite of our ignorance, we might be forgiven the sins committed against the Father who created us. It also showed that the relationship of Father and Son was fully intact in spite of His suffering.

Included in His intercession were prayers for Roman soldiers who were following orders, for Jewish authorities who viewed Him as a threat, and for Pontius Pilate who had the authority to release or kill Him. He forgave those who inflicted violence upon Him as well as those who jeopardized their own eternal destiny by their ignorance. In His words we see the arms of God open wide to receive the righteous and the unrighteous, anyone who would come. All—Jew and Gentile, religious and secular—could be taken into the embrace of the Cross.

While He prayed for the sinners of the world, the religious rulers mocked Him. The soldiers, also mocking, took His garments, His only possessions, and divided them among themselves. The crowd looked on in silence.

One criminal on the cross beside Him, though thoroughly deserving His judgment, asked to be delivered. He said, *"Lord, remember me when You come into Your kingdom"* (Luke 23:42). What did Jesus say? "No, I didn't mean you, you reprobate"? No, *"Jesus said to him, 'Assuredly, I say to you, today you will be with Me in Paradise'"* (Luke 23:43). This word of love promises eternal life to the criminal. A dying man saw the Christ being crucified beside him and chose to walk through the door of salvation. He embraced the mercy of God.

To him Jesus said, "It won't be some day far away; before the sun sets today I will have you with Me where I am in bliss." They were standing on the threshold between this life and the next, and He was (and is) there as both Doorkeeper and King, offering the only kind of release that matters.

It's amazing how we overlook the simple things Jesus said because they are so…simple. We tend to think spirituality is like religion: complicated and unpleasant.

Spirituality is breathing the Breath of God in and out. He told us "When you pray (assuming we would), don't do it to get people to notice your religion." (See Matthew 6:5.) He said, "When you pray, stand up; forgive; then get down to business!" (See Mark 11:25.)

In the novel, *The Shack*, the despair that is slowly eating away at Mack will only go away if he can find God as his Papa and forgive his enemy: "Forgiveness is first for you, the forgiver…to release you from something that will eat you alive; that will destroy your joy and your ability to love fully and openly."[1]

That day in my father's home when I stooped down to touch the place where the last of his life slipped away, I knew I had to forgive anybody and everything that had allowed this nightmare to become reality.

I had to have God's help to forgive like that, on the spot, before justice had been served. But I had the best help of all because Jesus is the One who personifies forgiveness.

On the Cross

The Cross is the story of forgiveness. The salvation of the world depends on it. Forgiveness is the simplest and yet most profound dynamic of human relationship, because love is impossible outside of it. Likewise joy is impossible outside of forgiveness.

But forgiveness is not a one-way street. There are two sides to effecting forgiveness. They are clear in the line from Jesus' model prayer: *"Forgive us our sins, just as we have forgiven those who have sinned against us"* (Matt. 6:12 NLT). These two sides are often overlooked in Christian experience. Most of us live our lives seeking God's forgiveness, but we fail to enter the state of grace through which we readily and fully forgive others. Unforgiveness holds two prisoners; the offender and the offended are equally bound. When the offended party extends forgiveness, the prison is opened and both offender and the offended go free.

The forgiveness Jesus teaches us is serious business. He gives what we give. He said the Father won't forgive us if we don't forgive others. God is an equal opportunity family man. He won't have a bunch of kids around Him who are play-acting at getting along and every time His back is turned they are tearing into one another or refusing to play together.

Jesus told His disciples that forgiveness is the first step of effective prayer. *"Whenever you stand praying, forgive, if you have anything against anyone, so that your Father also who is in heaven may forgive you your trespasses"* (Mark 11:25 ESV). We must be ready to extend the same degree of forgiveness that we anticipate receiving from the heavenly Father. Thus the praying Christian becomes a conduit of the power of salvation in the Cross.

Our voice in Heaven is only as loud as our forgiveness is deep. If you are experiencing a sense that the heavens are brass, that your prayers are not getting through, that you are ineffectual in your faith, check to see if you are holding unforgiveness in your heart.

The "Locks" of Forgiveness

Imagine a canal along which a ship passes through locks from one level to another. Along the canal the various locks regulate the flow of water.

If the men assigned to regulate the locks do not open them, the water cannot flow down and the ship cannot pass. The locks are forgiveness; the ship is salvation. You are a lockmaster, opening and closing the gates which allow the cleansing waters of the Spirit to flow. The river is the Spirit. Salvation can only flow as far as its recipients are willing to release it to others.

This river of life flows from the throne. It is the river flowing out of the city of God in John's revelation. Wherever this river flows, everything comes to life. But if it has no outlet, the water becomes a swamp, a swamp of unforgiveness. So when you stand praying, first forgive.

The obedient Son became your substitute on the Cross, making the exchange so that the rebel in you might be executed in Christ and that you might be born again and made righteous. Now you need to stretch your arms wide and release your forgiveness. Do you see those people mocking you? Forgive them. Do you see those people who just don't "get it," who persist in interfering with good things? Forgive them. Do you see those people who just won't agree with your point of view? Forgive them.

Jesus delivered us from self-centeredness when He shifted our focus to the true Center. Paul put it this way, and he pointed out what a transformational shift that represents in our lives:

Therefore, since we have this ministry, as we have received mercy, we do not lose heart. But we have renounced the hidden things of shame, not walking in craftiness nor handling the word of God deceitfully, but by manifestation of the truth commending ourselves to every man's conscience in the sight of God. But even if our gospel is veiled, it is veiled to those who are perishing, whose minds the god of this age has blinded, who do not believe, lest the light of the gospel of the glory of Christ, who is the image of God, should shine on them (2 Corinthians 4:1-4).

"Therefore…" Derek Prince always used to say, "When you see a 'therefore,' see what it's there for." Therefore, since you have received mercy, walk in righteousness—and in ongoing forgiveness—and the glorious light of Christ will shine out from your life.

FORGIVENESS RELEASES THE POWER TO SAVE

Surely you have heard the account of the martyrdom of missionary Jim Elliot and his four friends, Nate Saint, Roger Youderian, Ed McCully, and Peter Fleming. It happened in 1956, but the effects of that event will be felt for generations. It is a perfect example of the power of forgiveness.

While the story may be familiar, many of the details have been unknown.

The men had located a village of the Auca (now known as the Huaorani or Waodani) tribe near a jungle river, and had flown in to set up camp on a little sandbar in hopes of making contact with them. The tribe was known for their fierce infighting and hatred of outsiders. Their initial friendly contact ended in death—all five men were killed by spears within six days of setting up camp.

Suddenly five young wives were widowed and nine children were fatherless. Were the men foolish to have risked so much for a small group of primitive people whose every encounter with the outside world had ended in death—from the sixteenth-century conquistadors to seventeenth-century Jesuits to nineteenth-century explorers? The missionaries had prayed for years for this tribe. What good could come of their prayers now? What should the survivors do?

Their widows and other missionaries set the example: complete forgiveness. In spite of the magnitude of their losses and the ongoing dangers, some decided to stay in the jungle. Two of the women, Rachel Saint, the sister of Nate, and Jim Elliot's widow, Elisabeth, followed up directly with the tribe. When an opportunity arose, they moved to a village and worked to learn the Auca language, translate the Bible, and tell the Good News. Rachel ended up living with them for 37 years. Elisabeth went on to write books about her life with the tribe and much more, inspiring countless others to respond to the call to the mission field. Steve Saint, the son of Nate, grew up to become a missionary to the same country, and he became friends with his father's killers—all of whom became believers. According to Steve, the fact that the missionaries were capable of defending themselves (they had guns) and chose not to, was a major factor in the Huaorani men agreeing to allow his Aunt Rachel and Elisabeth Elliot to come live with them.

> They had to know the answer: why would the *cowodi* [foreigners] let themselves be killed rather than kill, as any normal Huaorani would have done? This question dogged Gikita [one of the tribesmen who was involved] until he heard the full story of why the men wanted to make contact and about another man, Jesus, who freely allowed his own death to benefit all people.
>
> Forty years ago, Gikita was an unusually old man in a tribe that killed friends and relatives with the same zeal and

134

greater frequency than they did their enemies. Now he is nearing 80 years of age and has seen his grandchildren and great-grandchildren grow up without the constant fear of spearings. He has repeatedly asserted that all he wants to do is go to heaven and live peacefully with the five men who came to tell him about Wangongi, creator God.[2]

The killers eventually spoke openly with Steve Saint about that day in 1956. "They knew that all of us have experienced God's forgiveness and that they had nothing to fear from me," wrote Steve.[3]

Yes, all of us have experienced God's forgiveness. Can we extend the forgiving grace of the Cross to the people around us, whether they are family, friend, or foe? Can we forgive freely so that we can pray freely—and with powerful results?

It seems almost too simple, and yet you know as well as we do that sometimes forgiveness can be nearly impossible. It seems counterintuitive. Why should you let a killer off the hook? Well, why not? Jesus did it first.

"For the message of the cross is foolishness to those who are perishing, but to us who are being saved it is the power of God" (1 Corinthians 1:18).

"And when we stand praying, as Jesus said, "we first forgive" (see Mark 11:25).

ENDNOTES

1. William P. Young, *The Shack* (Los Angeles: Windblown Media, 2007), 225.

2. Steve Saint, "Did They Have to Die?" Christianity Today, Sept 16, 1996, http://www.ctlibrary.com/861 from Susan Bergman, ed., *Martyrs: Contemporary*

Writers on Modern Lives of Faith, (San Francisco: Harper, 1996).

3. Saint.

CHAPTER 8

Safe From Ourselves, Safe From the Devil

Lead Us Not Into Temptation; Deliver Us From Evil...

EXPERIENCING DELIVERANCE AND PROTECTION.

In Madeira Beach, Florida, a group of tourists noticed something had gone wrong with two teenage girls who were parasailing together. They were drifting 250 feet in the air, not over the Gulf of Mexico, as they were supposed to be, but over the beach—and heading inland. The towline had snapped that had connected the girls to a boat in the Gulf. The girls were screaming. A man dove into the water to grab the line, followed by two more. They pulled with all their might in the waist-deep water, but the rope just slipped through their hands, searing their palms. The strong wind filled the parachute that was carrying the two girls perilously close to buildings and power lines. But then beachgoers got up off their towels and came streaming out of the condos to help. They grabbed onto the line and began to pull. Eventually as many as a hundred people were helping to bring the girls down safely to the beach. One of the girls said she was praying.

The powerful wind that that filled their sail had taken the girls captive. Even with the earnest effort of the first few people, the girls were still in great danger. It was only when the whole beach got involved—just as when the whole Church gets involved in corporate praying—that the victory could be claimed. They did not have enough power and strength until they banded together to exercise sufficient influence over an out-of-control situation.

In our culture, a whole generation can be blown away by powers of darkness if the Church doesn't hold on and drag them back to the solid, foundational truths of the Lord Jesus Christ. We need more than one or two people praying. The situation calls for hundreds of people holding onto the cord of prayer and agreeing in prayer. Together we can pull down the strongholds of darkness, resist the powers and principalities, and have the victory for our sons and our daughters.

Safe From Ourselves

Dr. Jekyll and Mr. Hyde is Robert Louis Stevenson's imaginative tale depicting the struggle between good and evil that wrests in the human heart.

Jekyll concocts a potion which will allow him to separate his good and evil personas in order to continue to be an upstanding Victorian man while doing the sinful acts denied a man of his social status. Thinking he could have the best of both worlds, he unwittingly embarks on a descent into hell. As the story unfolds we discover the respectable, affable humanitarian Dr. Jekyll and the hideous, deformed, violent Mr. Hyde are one in the same person. As Hyde and Jekyll each struggle for sole existence, terrifyingly, the horrible Hyde becomes more and more powerful and Jekyll is less and less able to control the dark side of his own nature. He says, "I knew myself, sold a slave to my original evil...every act and thought centered on self."[1]

The world thinks that "finding ourselves" leads us to discover what it means to be human. But the manner of the One in whose image humans are made is completely different. The three-personed God of Scripture is profoundly and infinitely self-giving. His glory is a shared glory, each delighting in the other. Christ did not humble Himself and take the form of a servant because He took on human flesh. He took on human flesh because He is a servant. We are *imago dei*, the image of God, created in Christ.

There are two enemies we face in the struggle to reflect God's glory in the earth. One is within and flows from the thoughts and imaginations of the human heart. It is inspired by the old man of sin, the corrupt human nature inherited from Adam and the Fall in Eden. The Bible calls this enemy our "flesh." The other enemy is also a person. Jesus faced him down during testing in the wilderness. Satan and his demons wield influence from without. Through principalities and powers they tempt, oppose, violate, kill, steal, and destroy. There is a way to safeguard both realms. That way is the way of the Cross. Through the Cross Jesus destroyed all the power of the devil and set the human soul free from its bondage to sin. Thus His prayer, "Lead us not into temptation but deliver us from evil." We enter into that victory, taking back the night and reclaiming territory formerly given over to the enemy by watching in prayer.

As we take up our cross in death to carnal passions God leads us in a parade of triumph and through us diffuses the fragrance of His knowledge in every place (see 2 Cor. 2:14).

The ultimate paradise of God is the heart of every human created in His image. When Jesus was tempted in the wilderness, it is clear that He kept watch over the gates of His heart, keeping Himself a garden where no seeds of the enemy could be sown to bring forth bitter fruit. Jesus testified to this when He said, *"...The ruler of this world is coming, and he has nothing in Me"*

141

(John. 14:30). Proverbs instructs, *"Keep your heart with all diligence, for out of it spring the issues of life"* (Prov. 4:23). It is toward the cultivation and keeping of the Eden of our hearts that we pray as watchmen awake in this hour, that God may have for Himself a land of pleasure in His new creation, created in Christ Jesus by the Spirit. We watch over them that our hearts might be cultivated with His Word and rained on by His Spirit. Keeping watch is not only observing regular communion individually and corporately through prayer; it is a lifestyle of joyful awareness of the Holy Spirit. Our quest together is to know God. That knowledge, that glory, that paradise was intended to reproduce itself under the watchful care of Adam and Eve until that abode covered the world and provided a habitation for their generations which were to come. We guard our hearts that out of them might come pure seed to be sown in the lives of our children and that they might arise after us to tend and keep until Christ comes. We hold God's promise that the knowledge of this glory will fill the whole earth (see Hab. 2:14). Adam and Eve faced a moral dilemma, not a physical one. There are two different kinds of hunger that we experience. We feed one with physical bread and the other with bread of a different nature. We see from the terrible tragedy of the choice made in Eden that "we are what we eat." When they ate of the tree from which God had said, abstain, death entered the entire human race. Eating of the tree of which God said "you shall not" resulted in autonomy from God and the entrance of death through sin. Conversely, becoming sons and daughters of obedience in Christ restores communion and life. Our "morals" are the orientation we possess toward understanding what is right and wrong, good and bad, worthy and unworthy, just and unjust. Good morals rest in a conscience awakened to Christ and formed by His truth.

C.S. Lewis said:

A thing may be morally neutral and yet desire for that thing may be dangerous...The painless death of a pious relative at an advanced age is not evil. But an earnest desire for her death on the part of her heirs is not reckoned a proper feeling, and the law frowns upon even the gentlest attempt to expedite her departure.[2]

To desire an inheritance coming from a grand old wealthy aunt is not in and of itself a bad thing. But to desire her untimely demise that you might receive the inheritance is a bad thing. In *Moral, Believing Animals: Human Personhood and Culture,* Christian Smith writes, "There's nowhere a person can go to escape moral order. There's no way to be human except though moral order."[3] Christians have a set of standards based in a relationship with an Influencer who anchors us, gives identity and trains our morality in His image. When Adam and Eve decided for themselves what was right and what was wrong, they hid from God. Because He loves us the Father searches us out asking, "Where are you?" (Gen. 3:9). Conscience is not something that allows us to justify doing whatever we want. It is not a mere "feeling" about what we should or should not do. *Conscience* is the judgment of reason whereby the human person recognizes the moral quality of a concrete act he is going to perform, is in the process of performing, or has already completed.

Conscience is the voice of God resounding in the human heart, revealing the truth to us and calling us to do what is good while shunning what is evil. A well-formed conscience doesn't come automatically or overnight. Conscience always requires serious attempts to make sound moral judgments based on the truths of our faith.

Awakening of Moral Conscience

Amidst the call for revival there must be a shofar for an awakening of the difference between right and wrong. This call takes us back to that old tree and the choice between satisfaction of man's urges according to his own knowledge or true freedom which comes

143

through aligning ourselves with the knowledge of God. The call for revival is a plea for renewal of the tested orthodoxy of our faith. That orthodoxy, the foundation of the Judeo-Christian worldview, is the ethic of hope for society. In his pastoral letter "Moral Conscience," retired Archbishop Harry Flynn wrote:

> The lack of a common intellectual and moral sense has contributed to a century of totalitarianism and materialism which converged to wreak havoc on all peoples and on the world we share. The result, however, has been more than a matter of global movements. On a smaller scale, these notions (which inevitably involve lies about God and man) are the basis also of individual moral decisions and values. Over time they have fostered a moral culture which prizes personal autonomy and subjective determination of good above all else, creating a world of "merely individualistic morality."[4]

Behavior follows heart attitude. As a man thinks in his heart, so is he. Out of the heart come the issues of life. We realize we all must get a new heart or we will die. With that new heart we need an invincible power source to renew and transform us. We are not defined by humanistic secular thinking or the wisdom of this present darkness. Through rebirth by faith in Christ we receive that invisible power source. His unstoppable Spirit provides a special kind of armor in our defense against evil as we battle to transform the darkness around us. The Church of Jesus Christ is God's last Act in the drama of human history. We are His "superfamily"— a unique spiritual creation placed here to usher in His unveiling. This is the assignment of watchmen.

We are unique because we have been born again. We are unique because we have been washed in the blood of Christ. We are unique because we have the Word of God. We are unique because we have received the Holy Spirit. This spiritual creation is realized in persons who form an eternal community through which God is bringing His story to a happily-ever-after conclusion.

The Champion will appear at a moment already set but yet to be unveiled.

Until then we must "act in the appropriate manner for this moment in the story; this will be in direct continuity with the previous acts (we are not free to jump suddenly to another narrative, a different play altogether)...We must be ferociously loyal to what has gone before and cheerfully open to what must come next"[5]

Safe From the Devil

I would that every man would lift up their hands and pray for all those in authority that you might live a peaceable and quiet life (see 1 Timothy 2:2,8). The Church is called to corporate prayer that we might serve as a spiritual vanguard in every nation. Wherever you are in the world, if you are a Christian, you have a commission and an anointing from Heaven to intervene and help direct and mold the governing factors in your nation. It begins in the Church with corporate watching and praying.

In ancient Israel, the watchtower that guarded a field, a city or a strategic point was called a mizpah. The watchtower was the point of vision and defense, day and night. Many important national and spiritual events occurred at the watchtowers. The Watch is a very practical tool of spiritual power. The government institutions are working to do all they can, but the Church has the responsibility to bring heaven down to intervene where the help of man is futile. Our watch prayers become vehicles of salvation, saving us from ourselves and from the wiles of the devil as we enter the realm of watchful expectation in faith—all our senses alert, our whole being alive unto the Spirit. The kind of spirituality needed in the new age of terror in the wake of 9-11 is hidden in the power of watching and praying. The whole world is concerned about terrorism now. This

145

danger is very real, and people are concerned for the safety of their families, their cities. Their sources of livelihood are being threatened. Now governments issue regular warnings of terror. It leads to a kind of debilitating inner terror, like the one Jesus and His disciples faced in the garden on the night He was betrayed. Armed men in ranks sought Him to kill Him. He watched, not because of the danger on earth, but in order that He might be fully aligned with the plan, purpose, and power of Heaven when that danger showed itself. Thereby, He could "fight" back in the strategy and with the armaments God ordained.

Early in the years of The Watch in Charlotte, North Carolina, one of our watchmen had a dream in which she saw our city with a wall around it much like the ancient cities whose walls created their defense from enemies. In the dream a sinister figure had sneaked inside and was carrying out evil schemes that threatened more than just the families in our town. We confirmed this impression was from the Lord and pursued it in prayer. Very specific prophetic information came to us over the next few hours. We began to sense that one of the operations in our town was financial support for Middle Eastern terror organizations. Specifically we knew the sinister force was a terror cell of Hezbollah which was networking with a wider scheme to harm innocent people here and abroad. This was long before the events of 9-11 awakened the world to the threat coming from radical Islam. In those days no one spoke of such things.

But as watchmen we were awake in prayer! We prayed for God to put together a successful interagency sting including FBI, INS, local police and others to find, capture, and root out this evil. When the burden lifted and we had prayed through, we celebrated in dancing and worship, giving God glory for the victory over this enemy that we had no natural ability to expose and capture. The following week, our city news released the story of a successful raid that exposed and broke up a Hezbollah terror cell in Charlotte.

Several years later, Fox News did a special on the story as part of their series on homegrown terror. The operation in Charlotte had been responsible for hundreds of thousands of dollars being funneled to buy weapons and explosives, enabling multiple acts of terror. The prophetic prayers of the watchmen awake in those hours played a strategic part in defeating darkness and bringing justice.

Pull Down Strongholds

I (Bonnie) had a dramatic experience that illustrates the power of the exercise of Heaven-delegated authority. Immediately after getting home from seeing the movie, *The Passion of the Christ*, I felt strongly led to go out on a prayer walk.

The night sky was clear and the splendor of the stars matched my re-inspired awe about Jesus' self-sacrificial love on the Cross. I was replaying scenes from the movie in my mind as I walked down the familiar street in our neighborhood. I thought about how Jesus' prayer in Gethsemane had been portrayed: as Jesus completed His surrender to the Father's will, He stood and took a single step—and the heel of His sandal crushed the head of a serpent.

I began to pray aloud in tongues, worshiping the Savior. Immediately, it was as if a veil was removed from my eyes, and I could see a mighty host of angels in the sky over my head. I could sense a mounted angel army coming on horses from Heaven, and it appeared that they were at my beck and call. I felt as though I were a vessel containing the incense of the watch prayers of the saints, and that my words of prayer could tip that vessel over and release Kingdom power into a situation. My mind turned to think about the flesh-and-blood soldiers who were serving overseas in the war on terror.

As soon as I thought about that, I was startled by a flash of light that seemed to arc from where I was standing and over the horizon to a military base where someone dear to us was currently stationed. We had prayed for him often, with much love, and now it seemed that all of those prayers had been bundled together and that a breakthrough was being achieved.

I had just reached an intersection in the road. At first I thought I was hearing the roar of some of those huge transport trucks coming up the highway, but when I turned toward the sound, it was a violent wind roaring through the valley in my direction.

I couldn't tell what direction the wind was coming from. I was being pelted with a combination of rain and debris that had been picked up by the wind. I braced myself against it, laughing in spite of the storm, because it seemed to be directly connected to my prayer—evidently this was the only response the "prince of the power of the air" could make to such a release of God's troops. There were no trucks. In fact, I didn't see any vehicles at all, and certainly not any other people.

Without thinking about how strange and even unsafe it was to remain outside in such a storm, I kept walking, singing Scripture at the top of my voice:

"The Spirit of the Lord God is upon me because He has anointed me to preach good news!" "This is the year of the favor of the Lord! This is the day of the vengeance of our God!" As I walked and sang, I saw two trees—it was a vision, I thought—and somehow I knew that those trees represented two particular evil afflictions of this generation of Americans. I walked right between the two trees, and, with great unction, declared words from the book of Jude: "You twice dead trees of perversion and rebelling I pull you up out of the heart and soul of America by the root." I reached my hand out toward each tree in turn to "uproot" them. I named the powers of deception and seduction and bound them in Jesus' name. Suddenly, a deafening crash caused all of the streetlights to go out.

Now in pitch blackness, I realized I was drenched, and I decided I really ought to head home. As I turned around, I thought I could see some car headlights through the lashing rain. The car pulled up to me; it was our daughter Serah who had come out into the storm to look for me. Gratefully, I got into the car, and as we turned around, I began to tell her about what had just happened. Just as I told her about the trees in my vision, our headlights scanned across two huge trees that had been uprooted and were lying across the highway. I had heard them being torn out of the earth by the wind as I was uprooting the spiritual "trees" in my prayer.

Safe at home, I told the rest of my family what had just occurred. The ring of the telephone interrupted me. Of all unexpected callers, it was the young soldier I had prayed for as I saw the arc of light shoot around the world to his military base.

"How are you able to call? Is something going on?" I asked.

"A little while ago," he said, "the power on the entire military base shut down. We got permission to come outside and use our cell phones while they try to restore power to our station."

I knew that God was giving a sign to all of us, to reinforce our faith that our faithful prayers can be that powerful. Attended by angelic armies, they perform the work of the Kingdom in delivering us from both unseen and seen evils.

Postscript: We went out in the morning to see what had happened in the storm. Sure enough, the two trees were still blocking the highway, and each was over seventy feet tall. More importantly, the following months brought powerful breakthroughs and a significant amount of transformation in the lives of some young people we had been praying for.

Honor Your Local Body of Christ

We wrestle not against flesh and blood, but against powers and principalities and dark authorities in heavenly places (see Eph. 6:12). "We" is the corporate body of Christ mobilized in local congregations and prayer meetings activated by the Spirit and faithfully keeping the light of the spiritual watchtower burning brightly in the night. It's corporate.

Wrestling is one of the most intense physical activities. Great expenditure of strength and endurance is required. Every muscle is used. There is a mental strategy and conditioning that must accompany the physical strength of the wrestler if he is to prevail. While we wrestle spiritual forces (not physical persons), the safety and well-being of physical persons is what's at stake when we take our place on the wall to watch and pray. Our necessary response to this wrestling match between the peace of God's kingdom and the power of darkness that threatens to take away peace in the world is described in M. Douglas Meeks' introduction to *Passion for God*:

> We live in a time of trembling and fear, when a sense of danger from which there is no escape can lead us to a numbness that is a kind of "death before death." This "paralyzing sleep" leads to a loss of a sense of reality so that we live only in our illusions. Jesus confronts us as he did His disciples in Gethsemane with the call to wake up out of our petrification.[6]

This new world condition requires a new way of praying. We must now pray with eyes on heaven, hands open in ready action and heads raised, alert to our world—It is the way Jesus prayed in Gethsemane when he was faced with terror. Moltmann described this prayer as, "Awakening, watching, and expectation are modes of prayer. We should pray with open eyes and hands because prayer means waking up to the world and perceiving the groaning of our fellow creatures. In order not to sink into a new abyss of despair we should discover the face of the crucified one in the face of the victims of violence. Prayer is at once participation in the sufferings of God and anticipation of the coming redemption of God"[7]

Like aerial warfare, we stand and send prayer rockets against evil forces attacking and keeping persons, families, cities, and nations bound. This is part of the mystery and the glory of watching and praying. But we are not lone snipers hidden in our prayer closets. We are companies, ranks, communities of light arising at midnight to turn back the enemy at the gates. Bless your local body of Christ by honoring all of its various parts and participants.

Without the Body of Christ, many of your prayers are barely audible in the spiritual realm. In terms of watching in prayer, it is corporate prayer that gets the best heavenly results. Just as it took the whole group of tourists on the Florida beach to pull down the runaway parasail, so it takes a unified prayer effort to pull down out-of-control forces of evil. By praying together, you will experience deeper revelation, more frequent prophecy and angelic activity, more healings and other answered prayers, and even atmospheric manifestations of the visitation of the Lord Himself. You need to belong to a local body of believers. You need the checks and balances of your brothers and sisters and the mentoring of those who are more mature in their walk of faith. To be useful, your spiritual gifts need to be fitted in with those of other members of the body. Don't spurn the people the Lord wants to combine you with; honor Him by honoring each other.

> "[Speak] *the truth in love,* [that you] *may grow up in all things into Him who is the head—Christ—from whom the whole body, joined and knit together by what every joint supplies, according to the effective working by which every part does its share, causes growth of the body for the edifying of itself in love*" (Ephesians 4:15-16).

Stand Your Ground

As we respond to the Lord daily and we pray individually and together, we will be able to *"withstand in the evil day, and having done all, to stand"* (Eph. 6:13). We can expect to be tested and tried in the process. It's as if we put His Word to the proof of personal experience.

The word "temptation" in the phrase, "lead us not into temptation" is *peirasmos* in Greek. That word has less to do with enticement through the sins of the flesh than it does with putting to proof through adversity. It's the same word that Paul used in Galatians 4:14 when he commended the church for receiving him in spite of his physical problem:*"And my temptation which was in my flesh ye despised not, nor rejected; but received me as an angel of God, even as Christ Jesus"* (KJV).

In Gethsemane, we see Jesus in the place of "temptation" where His obedience to His destiny was tested. These testings were the bookends of Jesus' earthly ministry, beginning with the Spirit's leading into the wilderness for a 40-day test, and ending with His victory in the garden as He bent His will to the will of the Father.

So when you pray "lead us not into temptation, but deliver us from evil," you're praying that you will be able to stand your ground against the forces of evil that pull at you. You are praying that God will keep His Bride from being misled or lured into the territory of the enemy, which is a land of lies, poverty of spirit, and broken character.

When Paul told the Ephesians, "Withstand in the evil day, and having done all, to stand," he had just finished telling them about putting on the armor of God for the spiritual battles they would face. We stand in Spirit-provided shoes that Paul compared to the sandals of a Roman centurion which were equipped with special spikes that allowed the soldier to dig in and not be pushed back. Corporately, the troops would link together and become an immovable human wall of resistance to the enemy onslaught. This is what we do in corporate watching prayer.

Awake in Prayer

"Watch" is a military word. There are three and sometimes four watches to every night. In the Bible, it was often in the fourth watch of the night that God would suddenly appear and rescue His people. From your position on the Rock, built on the Word, you can intercede for your children, your friends, and for everything that God draws to your attention. Intercession gives legs to your authority in Christ. Keep on interceding even when the subject of your intercession is far away from you. A watchman is God's sentinel bringing forth God's mercy and justice in the earth by the power of the Holy Spirit through prayer. The attitude of an awakened spirit, face up in expectation of Jesus, is the earliest prayer posture of Christianity. We see in the life of Jesus how a person becomes prayer and is able to "pray without ceasing."

In the Gospels as Jesus is going about His daily life, we find Him verbalizing His ongoing conversation with the invisible God. In a moment of human activity where supernatural intervention is called for, Jesus prays:

> *Abruptly Jesus broke into prayer, "Thank You Father, Lord of Heaven and earth. You've concealed Your ways from sophisticates and know-it-alls, but spelled them out clearly to ordinary people. Yes, Father, That's the way You like to work"* (Matthew 11:25-26 TM).

Jesus was awake in prayer. He lived watching in prayer. He drew his closest friends into His circle of prayer, and showed them how to fellowship with the Father together. He's still doing it today, and we are part of the ever-growing circle that is called the

153

Church. And as we watch and pray God's power for miracles and deliverance are released.

Sun Tzu, a famous military general from the 6th Century B.C. whose record of victory in battle is still studied by armies around the world said this: "If you know the enemy and know yourself, you need not fear the result of a hundred battles. If you know yourself but not the enemy, for every victory gained you will also suffer a defeat. If you know neither the enemy nor yourself, you will succumb in every battle." David faced many challenges as ruler in Israel. Enemies from without and weaknesses from within threatened to rob him and his nation of God's blessing. But David was awake in prayer. The post of watchman over his own heart and watchman over the house of Israel trained him to be able to bring deliverance from his enemies through his relationship with God wrought through unceasing prayer. In Psalms 109:1-4 we find his secret stated simply:

> *Do not keep silent, O God of my praise! For the mouth of the wicked and the mouth of the deceitful have opened against me; they have spoken against me with a lying tongue. They have also surrounded me with words of hatred, and fought against me without a cause. In return for my love they are my accusers, but* **I give myself to prayer** *(emphasis added).*

The literal translation of this phrase is "I AM" prayer. I am prayer. As we have said we learn to "be" prayer, to become incense going up to God, in contrast to acts of "doing" by rote repetition the things one traditionally finds associated with saying prayers. Jesus is I AM. I AM is prayer. Jesus is awake in prayer. He lived and lives watching in prayer. He draws his closest friends into His circle of prayer.

We observe three unique characteristics to Jesus' prayer in Matthew 11:

1. His ongoing inner conversation in communion with the Father would abruptly make its way to the surface to be heard in words from His mouth at any time. Verbal spontaneity of this prayer reveals His interior fellowship with the Father was unceasing. His prayer was constant. It was intimate, inward and verbal.

2. The first words were often "Thank You, Father." This depth of communion inspires worship and brings joy. It was formed out of praise and thanksgiving. It came from living conversation with and revelation through the Father.

3. The outflow was supernatural knowledge and wisdom readily present in all Jesus said and did, and with it came the absolute assurance that He had received what He had asked.

Intimate. Joyful. Revelatory. Answered. What a way to pray!

As watchmen of God take their place in the *mizpah* (watchtower) of His presence to watch and intercede, we appear before Christ to take our place with Him in His throne. Eyes of our hearts wide open in expectation and assurance, we are being changed from glory to glory into His image. And as we are changed we are being saved from ourselves and made safe from the devil!

ENDNOTES

1. Robert Louis Stevenson, *Dr. Jekyll and Mr. Hyde* (New York: Simon and Schuster, 2005), 74.

2. C.S. Lewis, *Weight of Glory: And Other Addresses* (New York: Harper Collins, 2001), 149.

3. Christian Smith, Moral, *Believing Animals: Human Personhood and Culture,* (New York: Oxford University Press, 2003), 8.

4. Archbishop Flynn, "Moral Conscience," May 20, 2008, http://www.zenit.org/article-22664?l=English.

5. N.T. Wright, *The Last Word: Beyond the Bible Wars to a New Understanding of the Authority of Scripture* (New York: Harper Collins, 2005), 123.

6. Jürgen Moltmann and Elisabeth Moltmann-Wendel, *Passion for God: Theology in Two Voices* (Louisville, KY: Westminster-John Knox Press, 2003), 10.

7. Ibid.

CHAPTER 9

You're in Charge

Yours Is the Kingdom...

STEPPING INTO THE FLOW OF *EXOUSIA*, THE BELIEVER'S KEY TO AUTHORITY.

As we have accepted the Lordship of Jesus Christ in our lives and are transferred from the kingdom of darkness into light, we have the privilege of coming under the headship of our King through a loving relationship with our Father. Intimate interpersonal relationship is the foundation of the flow of authority in the Kingdom of God.

Our faithful assistant, Heather, shares about a time when she came to the Friday night watch and the Lord underlined for her the reality of how it is *only* by a personal relationship with Him that somebody can step out in Kingdom authority:

I remember one Friday at the end of a challenging week, I came to The Watch in a bad mood and still wrestling with my reactions to some of the events of the week. I

159

knew that some things in my heart weren't exactly right in the way I was dealing with people, and I was carrying that as I got there and walked through the doors.

Once I was there, I just decided to participate in the worship; it wasn't really a very spiritual decision. I didn't feel anything except the hardness of my own heart. However, I opened my mouth and started to worship.

All of a sudden the Lord was right before my face. I was shocked. I don't mean I sensed His presence; I mean He was right in my face. It was like I could see the Lord, not really with my eyes, but with my spirit. He was right there to meet me and I was so surprised that I asked, "What are You doing here?" I really felt like I was in such a bad place that I would need to praise and worship and be all spiritual for a couple of hours before I could even think about actually meeting the Lord. It's funny how our minds work.

But in that moment it was as if the Lord rolled back all of my misconceptions of how we "earn" our way into relationship with Him. He was giving me a revelation of how we come into His presence, not by our actions or anything of our own merit, but through His righteousness and His justice and His blood that was shed on the Cross for us. That's how we boldly come before His throne and that's the whole purpose of our access.

Even though I had known that in my head, it was in that moment that the Lord shifted my entire internal perspective from something I knew but didn't quite have a full revelation of to something that just became part of me. I saw His pure mercy and love that are completely divorced from any merit of our own. Yes, I want to live a holy life, and I want to have the right attitude and I want to exemplify

Christ, but that's not what brings me into the presence of the Lord. It's His blood. As I stepped into a fresh revelation of the power and purpose of His blood it changed my perspective in my prayers for others. His blood not only allows me to come into His presence, but His blood gives me hope as I pray for our nation. His blood gives me authority to pray for people in desperate situations. It's His blood that lets me pray in faith for His purposes to come even when we don't necessarily deserve it. It's because of His blood and His mercy that we can ask Him to intervene because His blood is precious, and He paid the ultimate price so that those things would be for His glory and for His name and for His sake.

God rules in a family. God never intended for man to be ruled by any other than Himself. The pattern revealed from the very beginning was *sonship*, just as the Father delegated authority to Adam in the garden.

FATHER TO SON

The Godhead exemplifies the relational family nature in which God rules His Kingdom. Father is head of the Kingdom. He sent the Son in His name. Jesus was faithful in all the Father's will and so was given all authority. The Spirit has been sent in Jesus' name to be in and with every child born into the Kingdom in order that He might rule in their midst as resident Lord of the Church which is Christ's Body. This is how Christ came—the Father was in Him (see John 14:10).

The authority in which He moved was the result of the intimate personal relational connection. This was the same manner in which Adam the son of God was given dominion. God walked and talked with him in the garden in the cool of the day. Jesus likewise communed in fellowship with the Father, and as He did

161

so, He was instructed, corrected, and strengthened as a Son. As a result, He carried the weight of authority that God endued Him with.

Jesus Christ took back the Kingdom by completely laying down His own authority to the Father. In so doing He received all the authority of the Father and assumed complete dominion of Heaven and earth. When Christ sat down on high, the Father poured out His Spirit, fully God Himself and the third Person of the Godhead, bestowing the power and authority of the Kingdom as resident Lord of the Church on the earth. *"But as many as received Him, to them He gave the right* [exousia] *to become children of God..."* (John 1:12) The Holy Spirit administers the Kingdom with and in believers and He anoints persons with particular power and authority to rule His house.

Jesus' model prayer reveals God's objectives and priorities: "Yours is the Kingdom...." God's primary objective is for His Kingdom to be established on the earth; as a Son, Jesus learned obedience through the things which He suffered or endured as a servant, not doing His own will but the Father's. At the same time, while clothed in human flesh, Jesus had authority because he operated entirely under authority and instruction day to day: "The words are not Mine—they are the Father's. The works are not Mine—they are the Father's" (see John 14:10).

KINGDOM AUTHORITY

The Gospel of salvation concerns the restoration of the Kingdom under God with Christ as King. Jesus Christ is called King of kings and Lord of lords.

A kingdom indicates a particular realm having a king, a throne, subjects, and a governing jurisdiction. According to the Bible at this present time all of creation is divided into two kingdoms, the Kingdom of light and the kingdom of darkness. Both kingdoms are spiritual and both have heads: God and the devil.

Jesus said, *"My kingdom is not of this world"* (John 18:36), meaning that worldly authorities did not give Jesus His Kingdom and they cannot take it away. Jesus' Kingdom is seated in the spiritual realm and its power is extended in the natural realm. The Kingdom of God is a Kingdom of power and authority.

There are two Greek words that were sometimes interchanged in the King James Version of the Bible, but they are different from each other. In Greek, the word for "power" is *dunamis*. That is where we get our English word, *dynamite*. But the Greek word for "authority" is *exousia*. We often focus only on *dunamis* power, but authority, or exousia is its twin. For full effect, they must operate together.

Jesus preached a message of authority proven by miraculous acts of power:

> *Now when He came into the temple, the chief priests and the elders of the people confronted Him as He was teaching, and said, "By what authority are You doing these things? And who gave You this authority?"* (Matthew 21:23).

> *And they were astonished at His teaching, for He taught them as one having authority, and not as the scribes* (Mark 1:22).

> *Then they were all amazed, so that they questioned among themselves, saying, "What is this? What new doctrine is this? For with authority He commands even the unclean spirits, and they obey Him"* (Mark 1:27).

> *And they feared exceedingly, and said to one another, "Who can this be, that even the wind and the sea obey Him!"* (Mark 4:41).

The Kingdom of God is manifest in our realm today in signs and wonders to break the bondage of the devil over mankind. It became manifest for the first time when Jesus walked the earth. His words were accompanied with confirming signs and wonders of healing and deliverance from demons, the indication of the authority to loose people from satanic rule of oppression. *"But if I cast out demons by the Spirit of God, surely the kingdom of God has come upon you"* (Matt. 12:28).

Kingdom Authority in Action

So often, it's simple cause and effect: in the presence of the Kingdom of God, His authority causes miracles to occur—even if we are reluctant to participate, as I (Mahesh) was once when I was ministering at an event where Dave Wilkerson's group, Teen Challenge, had gone out and brought in people off the streets.

There I was standing with the microphone and there they were in the front row—twelve drug-addicted prostitutes in their "trade outfits"—the shortest skirts you can imagine, etc. I didn't know where to direct my eyes, and I really didn't want them to be sitting right there in front of me like that.

Wouldn't you know, when I gave the invitation, the very first ones to stand up to get saved were these twelve prostitutes. So I said a standard prayer, a repeat-after-me prayer, "Lord Jesus, I repent of my sins and I turn my back on the kingdom of darkness and I renounce the devil," and so forth.

These twelve were weeping; mascara was dripping down their faces. And I was just keeping my eyes closed as much as possible because I just couldn't look at them. Then I began to hear thuds and I opened my eyes and all twelve were on the floor, crying and speaking in tongues. I hadn't even gotten to that part yet.

Now I was keeping my eyes open, watching what was happening. With their revealing outfits, nobody could miss the fact that most of them were heroine addicts with visible needle marks on their skin. Suddenly, right before our eyes, every needle mark disappeared! God was renewing and restoring them as His daughters, delivering them from drugs instantly as they came into His presence. The power of the Kingdom had been released into their lives instantly; that's how the One with Kingdom authority had manifested Himself.

Jesus, the Son who carried the ultimate authority of God, has given us His Spirit. Now the Church is the body which God is anointing to advance His Kingdom.

Disciples of Christ receive authority as they are relationally connected to the Head and extend the Kingdom by *exousia* and *dunamis*. This is what is meant by "Go in My name and I will be with you." *"In My name"* literally means "instead of Me" or "in the same manner as My envoy, representative, messenger, or ambassador." Christians are to be the personal messengers of Christ Himself in every situation.

The Believer's Key to Power—Becoming a Disciple

The basic authority for the activity of the Church is the final instruction of Christ to His disciples. We're almost too familiar with what we call the Great Commission. Our familiarity with it makes us miss a key phrase: "make disciples":

> *Jesus came and spoke to them, saying, "All authority has been given to Me in heaven and on earth. Go therefore and make disciples of all the nations, baptizing them in the name of the Father and of the Son and of the Holy Spirit, teaching them to observe all things that I have commanded you; and lo, I am with you always, even to the end of the age"* (Matthew 28:18-20).

The majority of the world's population today could appropriately be viewed exactly as Jesus saw the multitudes after having taught and healed them: "like sheep without a shepherd." The world is dying for the disciples of Christ to do what they have been given to do. The only prescription for the moral and spiritual bankruptcy of the world is these last words of Jesus. They emphasize active proclamation of the Gospel message: *Go* with the assignment to *make disciples* of *all* persons, not having prejudice against anyone, *baptizing* them and *teaching* them to observe all Jesus commanded—and doing this with Him present!

The purpose of preaching is to extend the Kingdom of God through salvation, *but the fruit of salvation in an individual's life is discipleship.* In salvation we die to ourselves and take on the image and nature of Christ Himself.

Christian discipleship, rebirth and transfer from the kingdom of darkness into the Kingdom of light, is the ultimate remedy for the ills of society brought on as a result of the Fall of Man and subjection to the dominion of Satan. From personal failure to international terror, Jesus is the answer.

But What *Is* a Disciple?

"Disciple" comes from the Latin *discipulus,* a student. A disciple is a convert, but not all converts are disciples. By definition, disciples have to be "in process." They are lifelong learners. They sit at the feet of their Teacher, and they pay attention to what He says.

Jesus, even as the Incarnate Son of God, was a disciple before He was anything else. The Bible points to the essential nature of His "learning obedience" as a son, which is the essence of discipleship. He said, *"I do nothing of Myself; but as My Father taught Me, I speak these things"* (John 8:28). He studied under Pharisee tutors of the Torah and served an apprenticeship as a carpenter's son until He was 30 years old. Jesus submitted to all natural authorities including paying the taxes required by the state. He remained under direct daily authority and obedience to the Father throughout His life, receiving instruction, and direction until the time He was glorified.

His greatest ministry moment was the act of ultimate obedience to the will of another. It was His moment of greatest authority and most effective ministry. He went to the Cross, not of His own volition, but according to God's will. It was *after that* that the Son of Man was raised up to sit on the throne having all things put in subjection under His feet. Before that, Jesus had authority because He was under authority!

By definition, a *disciple* is one who is under the discipline of another. A disciple knows and is known and has come under the command of the one discipling him or her. A disciple of Jesus is a permanent, accountable, contributing member of a local church assembly under the authority of their local church leaders. God has given us the model for His family and government on the earth—His Church. Being a disciple begins with the simple step of becoming a member of a local body of believers.

Being a disciple comes from personal association as a student. The first disciples were known as having been with Jesus: *"Now when they saw the boldness of Peter and John, and perceived that they were uneducated and untrained men, they marveled. And they realized that they had been with Jesus"* (Acts 4:13). This principle challenges cyber- and long-distance mentoring. Discipleship is caught as well as taught.

Being a disciple necessitates that we give up what we are in exchange for what He would have us to be, taking up the cross to follow Christ in all things:

> *Now great multitudes went with Him. And He turned and said to them, "If anyone comes to Me and does not hate his father and mother, wife and children, brothers and sisters, yes, and his own life also, he cannot be My disciple. And whoever does not bear his cross and come after Me cannot be My disciple"* (Luke 14:25-27).

Discipleship includes following a lifestyle and being conformed to a way of thinking and acting. *Serving* is as important for training and impartation as lesson study. We see from the example of Elijah and Elisha that although there were a multitude of schools of the prophets in the cities of Israel at that time, Elisha received the mantle of a double portion of the spirit that was on the prophet Elijah through the practical service of running his errands, emptying his chamber pot every morning, and cooking and cleaning for him. That's what opened the way for Elisha to receive the blessing of being an empowered disciple.

Discipleship requires taking the position and nature of a bond slave and includes subjecting your will to that of another.

> *But Jesus called them to Himself and said, "You know that the rulers of the Gentiles lord it over them, and those who are great exercise authority over them. Yet it shall not be so among you; but whoever desires to become great among you, let him be your servant. And whoever desires to be first among you, let him be your slave"* (Matthew 20:25-27).

This service cannot be imposed, but is the heart attitude and position of those who willingly set their hearts on aligning themselves to their King.

Did you know that there is no biblical foundation for being "led by the Spirit" without the input and oversight of recognized spiritual authority? When novices and believers act independently of the counsel of those appointed as overseers in their lives they endanger themselves and others. Not even the apostle Paul presumed to go his own way without seeking the counsel of the rest of the elders and leaders God had placed over him in the church (see Acts 13:2-3).

Finally, being a disciple requires *faithfulness "He who is faithful in what is least is faithful also in much"* (Luke 16:10).

Timothy is a good example. He was taught and trained at home in the Word and ways of God (see 2 Tim. 1:5; 3:14-15). He proved himself in faithful service within his local church assembly (see Acts 16:1-2) and then he was chosen to work with Paul and learn from him (see Acts 16:3-4). After a time, Paul left him in Ephesus to teach proper doctrine as he had learned it from Paul, and Paul continued to oversee him (see 1 Tim. 1:3). Sent to Corinth and Philippi as Paul's representative, he dealt with things the way Paul himself would have done (see 1 Cor. 4:17 and Phil. 2:19-23). After a long time, he was left on his own to train others as he had been trained (see 2 Tim. 3:10).

Timothy proved himself over and over as a faithful disciple of the Lord Jesus. Most likely he supported himself in some manner, as Paul did also. So too must each of us work to support ourselves and to further improve our faithfulness. A good work ethic is a primary indicator of someone who is a good citizen of the Kingdom of God. (Note: One of the greatest potential hindrances to the strength of the Kingdom is the notion that so many people are called into full-time itinerant ministry. This is an unscriptural doctrine in the contemporary Church culture. All except those who have been raised up by the local church have been commended by God to work to support themselves and their families. See 2 Thessalonians 3:7-10.)

KINGDOM COMMUNITY

The vitality of early Christianity was spawned in the interaction of community. The disciples' common life together enabled the Word of God to be spoken in a rich variety of forms, from teaching to prophecy, producing an extraordinary awareness of God, which created practical change in their personal life.

In his book, *Hungry for God,* Ralph Martin writes:

It is clear from Scripture that God's fundamental intention is that we approach union with Him and a life of prayer not as our personal burden, but rather as a concern shared by the community of which we are a part. God's plan for our approach to Him is essentially communal. As we open up to the Holy Spirit, we need to open up to being drawn from what for many of us is a highly individualistic form of life to an increasingly community-oriented form of life. As our commitment to Him grows, His intention is that our commitment to one another grows. As we love Him more and more, His intention is that we love one another more and more. Loving God and loving our neighbor are, for a Christian, part of the same call.[1]

The heights of watching in prayer are experienced as a communal event. John saw the highest heights of communal ecstasy in the great company surrounding the Lamb's throne. Paul described this great oneness of prayer: *"You have come to Mount Zion and to the city of the living God, the heavenly Jerusalem, to an innumerable company of angels, to the general assembly and church of the first-born who are registered in heaven, to God the Judge of all, to the spirits of just men made perfect"* (Heb. 12:22-23). The "you" Paul was speaking to was a whole church congregation. Every Christian is called to be a part of a community of believers.

We are living in a day and hour that necessitates the power and authority imbued in corporate prayer. Jesus went "as was his custom" into the mountain to pray during the night watches. He would take with Him two or three of His watchmen friends. It is recorded that those friends were regularly James, John, and Peter. By being with Him and having not just been taught by Him, Jesus' disciples carried the same *exousia* and *dunamis* as He did. The Sanhedrin saw the bold preaching of Peter and John and they perceived them to be men who had been with Jesus because they carried themselves with such a new spirit of life and authority that even their enemies sensed it.

So it is for us.

The Lord is with us as we watch in prayer and we step into the flow of His exousia from the throne, declaring, "Yours is the kingdom."

ENDNOTE

1. Ralph Martin, *Hungry for God: Practical Help in Personal Prayer* (Ann Arbor, MI: Servant Publications, 2006), 98.

CHAPTER 10

Dunamis

Yours Is the…Power…

BRINGING IN THE POWER OF PENTECOST.

The headline said, "Bloody Burglar Defeated by Child."

A little girl in Colorado woke up early one Saturday morning to find a blood-covered stranger standing over her bed. Instead of being scared, she said she was mad.

If you were sleeping in your bedroom and suddenly you woke up to see a stranger looking down at you, covered in blood, what would you say? Probably something like, "Ahhh!" And yet instead of being scared, this young girl said she was mad because, "He can't put blood in our house." So the five-year-old, who stood less than four feet tall, escorted the burglar to the back door and told him, "Get out of my house."

As it happened, the police had been called already because this man had broken into another home in the neighborhood, so when Jacqueline opened the door and said, "Get out of my house," the burglar walked into the arms of the police.

Little children shall lead us.

On the original Palm Sunday, children were extolling Jesus as the Son of David, and the officials objected:

> But when the chief priests and scribes saw the wonderful things that He did, and the children crying out in the temple and saying, "Hosanna to the Son of David!" they were indignant and said to Him, "Do You hear what these are saying?"

> And Jesus said to them, "Yes. Have you never read, 'Out of the mouth of babes and nursing infants You have perfected praise'?" (Matthew 21:15-16)

Jesus was quoting from a psalm of David:

> O Lord, our Lord,
> How excellent is Your name in all the earth,
> Who have set Your glory above the heavens!
> Out of the mouth of babes and nursing infants
> You have ordained strength,
> Because of Your enemies,
> That You may silence the enemy and the avenger" (Psalms 8:1-2).

First David extols the glory of God: "You have set Your glory above the heavens." And then immediately following he says, "Out of babies' mouths You have established strength because of Your foes to still the enemy." Glory! Exalt Him to the highest! He is the greatest! No one can be wiser, stronger, greater!...And *babies*! The contrast is stark.

Babies are weak. They don't have much knowledge. Babies are utterly dependent on their mommies and their daddies, on others. In the world's eyes, they are insignificant. So why did God put them here? What are they doing? "Babies." That's not the answer we are looking for. Why did Jesus use a quote about babies on Palm Sunday? Because the babies were exalting His name. By opening their mouths, they were actively defeating the enemies of God, bringing the enemies of God to a standstill. The more humble position you take, like a child, the more your foes will be defeated. God's rule is established through humble servanthood. And the King of Glory was riding into the city on a donkey.

It was His triumphal entry into Jerusalem. Jesus was at the culmination of His earthly life and ministry. It was His last week on earth, and Jesus quoted Psalm 8, which shows us what the majesty of God implies in our lives. Jesus was focused on this aspect in His triumphal entry. The two words for "Lord" in "O Lord, our Lord" are not the same in Hebrew. The first one is a translation of the name "Yahweh." It's the personal name of Israel's God, built on the statement in Exodus 3:14: "I AM who I AM."

God spoke His name to Moses out of the burning bush. Moses replied, "Who are you?"

God answered, "I AM who I AM." God named Himself. He is the absolutely existing One, the One who did not come into being. Nobody made Him and so He cannot go out of being. He never changes His *being-ness*, because He is absolute being. He depends on nothing else for His being. He doesn't need oxygen, doesn't need food. He is the self-existent One.

Everything else depends on Him. Your every breath depends on Him. Every aspect of your life depends on "I AM who I AM," Yahweh. The more you recognize and acknowledge and open yourself to Him in all his majesty, the more the blessing you will receive. The more congruent your life is to this "I AM who I AM," the more His majesty will dwell and shine out through you. "O Lord, our Lord, How excellent is Your name in *all* the earth."

There is therefore no place in the earth where the Lord is not Yahweh, where He is not God. He is the absolute One in Moscow. He is the absolute One in Baghdad. He is the absolute One in Kabul. He is the absolute One in New York City. He is the absolute One in Washington, DC. Everything everywhere depends on Him. He has no competition. He is greater, wiser, more beautiful, more wonderful than everything everywhere. Lord, Master, King, Ruler, and Father of all who call on Him in truth.

God has His act together and the more we worship Him, the more we get in tune with Him, the more we experience who He is.

In the psalm, David goes on to describe God, the Creator:

When I consider Your heavens, the work of Your fingers, the moon and the stars, which You have ordained, what is man that You are mindful of him, and the son of man that You visit him? (Psalm 8:3-4)

Good question. Why should the Almighty care for human beings? Why is this "man" mentioned here?

He is here so that he can take dominion over the works of God's hands. *"You have made him to have dominion over the works of Your hands; You have put all things under his feet"* (Ps. 8:6). So God uses even babies and children to defeat His foes. He uses people to rule His glorious creation. He rules the world with the weakness of human beings. The glory of God's strength is greater because it is established through human weakness. His strength is magnified in your weakness.

Hudson Taylor wrote, "The power of prayer has never been tried to its full capacity. If we want to see mighty works of Divine power and grace wrought in the place of weakness, failure disappointment, let us answer God's standing challenge, 'Call unto Me, and I will answer thee, and shew thee great and mighty things, which thou knowest not [Jer. 33:3 KJV].'"

FROM AUTHORITY TO POWER

In the previous chapter, we talked about how our authority in Christ works. Jesus told His disciples, *"Behold, I give you the authority to trample on serpents and scorpions, and over all the power of the enemy, and nothing shall by any means hurt you"* (Luke 10:19). After giving His authority to the twelve, then to the seventy, He then gave authority to *all* His disciples when He said, *"All authority has been given to Me in heaven and on earth. Go therefore and make disciples..."* (Matt. 28:18-19).

That's the *dunamis*, that's the power—"ye shall receive power" (Acts 1:8 KVJ). We combine *dunamis* with *exousia*. People think they need only *dunamis*, but to receive *dunamis*, we have to be men and women who are under authority. We have to be like the centurion who said to Jesus, "I am a man under authority, and therefore I can say 'Go,' and these soldiers will go," (see Luke 7:8). You recognize Jesus as your premier authority.

God wants to raise up an army of men and women who have both dunamis and exousia, with excellence in anointing.

To understand authority and therefore true power, you need to understand the army idea. If you're going to be part of God's *exousia-dunamis* army, you cannot be a Lone Ranger. You have to be linked with others, and you have to be under the authority of someone who can impart it to you. I (Mahesh) had a miracle ministry years before, but I felt I had to submit my life and come alongside and serve a spiritual father: I found one in Derek Prince.

Spiritual fathers and mothers have mantles of authority, apostolic mantles. When you come alongside and pay the price of being servants, becoming a man or a woman under authority, learning, then the authority will start to be imparted. It will just start coming into your innermost being. In time, you will become what I call a "strong point of victory," part of one of the colonies of Heaven that God is establishing on the earth.

God is looking to set up His colonies of glory wherever His name is named. It doesn't happen with just a wave of the hand, but God wants to inject you with His presence, His authority, and His anointing, so that you can become a strong point.

The Church has had too much empty noise and God wants to give us substance. He wants to anoint you with fresh oil.

Fresh Oil

Oil of the anointing of the Spirit on Jesus flows down to those who hold Him as Head and King. Anointing oil in Scripture has three ministrations: (1) for healing; (2) for consecration of priests; and (3) for anointing of kings. In the Church, these three are equivalent to the anointing for: (1) miracles; (2) spiritual ministry, including the gifts of the Spirit; and (3) governing power, beginning with the five-fold ministries.

Jesus has been given as Head over all things to the Church in the same way a physical body receives life and direction from being connected to its head: *"He is the head of the body, the church, who is the beginning, the firstborn from the dead, that in all things He may have the preeminence"* (Col. 1:18). Just as the head is necessary for the body to function properly for life, in the same way one under authority receives direction and life-sustaining power. To be disconnected from the Head means you cease to receive revelation; you are disabled; your life ceases. In order to receive life, there must be a living connection to the head of the body. For revelation, life, and activity to occur in the body, all members—skeletal, muscular, vascular, cellular—must be in their proper places, functioning well together.

Not all body parts are connected by placement directly to the head. In fact the majority of the body members are directly connected to other members that eventually connect with the head but this means that the member-to-member relationship is vital for the supply of the head to flow down. Christ, our Head, has placed apostles, prophets, pastors, teachers, and evangelists anointed according to the measure of the Holy Spirit's administration to equip the saints for the work of ministry.

The authority to pray effectively comes from the Head and flows down as we are connected to Jesus, who says, "In My name you can cast out demons, heal the sick, release captives, preach good news, proclaim God's favor, be delivered from the enemy (and if you drink any deadly thing it shall in no wise harm you)" (see Mark 16:17-18). Jesus indicated that the anointing of the Holy Spirit would empower His messengers even over nature in the preaching of the Gospel.

During one of our campaigns in Africa, I (Bonnie) was served an unidentified drink that our team was certain should have been deadly, but it had no negative effects to my body. We were grateful for the anointing that comes to us through the Great Commission. That's power, not just in word, but also in deed. Essentially, we each become like a "little Jesus," manifesting in the earth as "sent ones" with the mantle of His authority.

The secret to moving in more of the healing anointing is connection to the Head. Jesus' robe was the point of contact for the woman with the issue of blood (see Matt. 9, Mark 5, and Luke 8). She took hold of Jesus by holding onto those little knots called *tzit-tzit* on the corners of His *tallit*. She connected there and literally turned His head in her direction so that healing virtue went out of Him to cleanse and restore her. The robe had nothing to do with the miracle except to be connected to the Head from which miracles flow. The world is bowed over like that woman who was sick for so many years. When she touches us, will she be healed because we are receiving the fullness of the oil that flows down from the Head?

Power is the primary element of spiritual advancement and extension of the Kingdom of God. In Scripture, power is associated with authority, miracles, dispossession of demonic strongholds, and possession of spiritual inheritance. *"You shall receive power when the Holy Spirit has come upon you; and you shall be witnesses to Me"* (Acts 1:8). Spiritual power is given to believers in order to show forth Christ, to testify of Him in word and deed. This is the Great Commission.

Deliverance

In the authority of this Great Commission, Jesus released the power of His name for miracles to demonstrate the advancing heavenly Kingdom through the Church until He comes. *"And these signs will follow those who believe: In My name they will cast out demons…"* (Mark 16:17). The deliverance ministry of the Church is primal to her demonstration of the Kingdom of God. When Jesus cast out demons, He said, "My kingdom has come."

Deliverance has been a big part of my (Mahesh's) ministry from its early years in Texas. When I was just starting out as a young man and had just been filled with the Holy Spirit, already there were people being set free, not only getting miracles and healings, but being set free from demonic oppressions. There were a lot of people who were calling me. I was based in Texas, because I was finishing graduate studies at Texas Tech University. I was so busy, I got only a few hours of sleep a night, because the people were just hungry to get a touch.

One night, I had gone to bed around three o'clock after driving about two hours back to Lubbock where I lived. I was so tired; I went to sleep. At around 7:30 in the morning, I got this call when I was still sleeping. It was a group of pastors who met together to pray and do some ministry, and they told me, "Brother Mahesh we need your help! Please come; it's an emergency."

I said, "What emergency?" Man, I was so tired. I didn't want to go anywhere.

They said, "We were praying for someone and the demon is talking back to us."

I said, "Well cast it out."

They said, "Brother Mahesh, please don't argue with us. We are scared."

I said, "You are Pentecostal, charismatic pastors. Cast it out yourselves."

They said, "Please, we are so scared."

So I relented. "All right, tell me where you are."

They told me where to come. So I got out of bed, got dressed, and went to find this place. They had told me, "When you come, please come by the back door."

So I went to the back door, went in, and heard this scuffling behind a door. I opened the door and it was kind of a laundry room, and there were eight pastors hiding in there.

I said to them, "What are you doing here?"

They said, pointing, "Because *he's* out there."

I shook my head, and went out to the other room and there was this very big man sitting in a chair. They had been praying and the demon had come to the surface and was talking to them, and it was a demon of sexual perversion. When he saw me he said, "Oh, you are pretty."

My hair stood up. It was another voice, and the thing started growling, and animal noises started coming out, and he said, "Come here. I want to have fellowship with you."

I felt like I needed to go take a bath or something. But the Holy Spirit came on me and so I said, "You want fellowship with me? You want me to tell you what the Bible says? First John 1:7 says that *'if we walk in the light as He is in the light, we have fellowship with one another, and the blood of Jesus Christ His Son cleanses us from all sin.'* And since you began to talk about fellowship, now I'm going to finish this conversation. I insist right now, since you talked about fellowship, let me finish the sentence, it is the blood of Jesus that cleanses us from all sin. So, demon, I want you to confess right now that the blood of Jesus cleanses from all sin, the blood of Jesus..."

And that thing came to the surface, and it started screaming, and the man's bones started twisting. His bones started shaping themselves into things no human can naturally do.

I said, "Shut up. Stop that. Get out of him."

And he came out screaming; the demon came out and left that man.

About fourteen years later, I came through that area again, and I heard a knock on my hotel room door, and lo and behold it was that very man. He said, "Brother Mahesh, I heard you were in the city, and I wanted to just come and thank you. That day I was delivered completely. I want to introduce you to this woman that I married a year later. I have normal desires, and I have a wonderful family. Thank you for praying for me."

That's the power that comes from our authority in Jesus.

The Word in Power

We need language to express this authority and to see its power. Did you notice how I used the Word of God in that situation?

The Bible is the Word of God. It is alive, active, full of power. God, our Father, speaks to us through His Word and we are not confused. Faith comes by hearing and hearing by the Word of God.

Every time you get into the Word, you can know there is divine, *dunamis* power at work. The Holy Spirit is going to be doing something. Junk will be falling away. You will be getting delivered. Healing will be coming to you, along with restoration.

God has loaded His Word with benefits for you. So don't come lethargically; come with expectation.

First and foremost, *read* the Word of God. Our spiritual father, Derek Prince, was a man who ardently loved his Bible. He used to remark, "A man's relationship with Jesus will be reflected in his relationship with his Bible." Christ is revealed through His Word. The Holy Spirit uses the Word to wash and sanctify us. The Word creates faith in our hearts. The Word sharpens our spiritual awareness and matures us. The Word provides sustenance.

The Bible is the most unusual book ever written. Even though written thousands of years ago, when we read it the Author still comes and looking over our shoulders begins to break it open that we might receive life. We recommend that you have more than one translation on hand if possible. Many contemporary Christians read only modern language versions for their simplicity. Unfortunately many of them, while conveying a sense of what the Author wrote, do not convey a clear revelation of many important truths. If you have difficulty reading your Bible regularly, we suggest starting by putting your Bible by your bed, so you can read it for a few minutes a day.

As you read, *think* about what you are reading. Choose a verse or a line from the daily portion you have just read. Turn the words over in your mind in the same way you would savor something delicious to eat. Allow the Holy Spirit to illumine particular words or thoughts in the phrase. Let those words find a connection with where you are at the moment. Now take the words with you as you go about your day. Bring them back to mind; allow the Holy Spirit to embed them in your heart. Immediately you will experience two things. One is a sense of peace that the Word creates for your mind, and the second is a sense of joy the Word brings to the heart. We've also found that these same meditations come alive as powerful prophetic prayers when we watch in prayer.

Now let yourself hear the word you've been thinking on. Sing it, declare it, pray it, make it stereophonic. Angels move, demons tremble, and God draws near as the Word makes a sound. The great watchmen in the Bible, Ezekiel and Daniel, created history with the words of God they spoke aloud. When you utter them, the words of the Word charge the atmosphere and come even more alive and active and full of power.

His Word is alive as we are. His Word is active as we are. And it is full of power as we are filled with His Spirit.

A great tool in developing your deeper life in Christ as you read, think, and say the Word of God is your prayer language. Pray in the Spirit as you read the Word, as you think about the Word, and as you begin to pray the Word out loud. It is like adding oil to machinery and gasoline to a fire.

"And these signs will follow those who believe:…they will speak with new tongues…" (Mark 16:17). One of the greatest gifts of empowering for the Church for her prayers, her proclamation of the Gospel, and her empowerment to demonstrate the Kingdom, is the gift of speaking in tongues (see Acts 2:4). We call it the mother tongue of Heaven. This mysterious equipping has been too long maligned, debated, disdained, and dragged through the mud.

Do you want empowering by the Spirit? Do you want a fresh river of revelation? Do you want deeper intimacy with God?

Receive the gift of speaking in tongues. The apostle Paul said, "I pray in tongues more than you all" (see 1 Cor. 14:18). Like miracles of healing and deliverance from demons, the gift of speaking in tongues is a manifestation of the presence of the Holy Spirit that glorifies God. Paul was not scandalized by this very practical ministry tool; it came in handy more than once during his apostolic journeys.

For centuries, monks have used the pauses in their reading of the Word for mental prayer, which they call "becoming prayer." These pauses provide times wherein the soul can become one with the words and raise itself to God, uniting to His will. In that place, the illumination shining on the heart from the nearness of His presence unveils the imperfections of the heart. This experience of being prayer is like the coals and incense on the ancient golden altar that stood before the veil. In the immediacy of the moment, dissonance in our hearts resounds like an out-of-tune instrument and repentance is the only appropriate response to God's revealed presence. Meditative, Word-based "becoming prayer" allows us to get in tune with God. We have talked very little about the posture of our prayers. We find that action helps. Try standing up in addition to kneeling down when you pray. Don't always lie facedown in travail—turn over and pray face-up, singing instead of speaking the words of your heart. Don't always fold your hands together, bow your head, close your eyes. Instead, try hands open and raised up, face up and eyes open. These actions depict the change in your attitude toward prayer. These are postures of *expectancy* and faith. They will affect the posture of your heart as well.

My House Is a House of Prayer

After Jesus went into the temple of God and drove out all those who bought and sold in the temple and overturned the tables of the money changers and the seats of those who sold doves, He said to them, *"It is written, 'My house shall be called a house of prayer,' but you have made it a 'den of thieves'"* (Matt. 21:13). Then the blind and the lame came to Him in the temple and He healed them.

Notice here that Jesus cleanses the temple and then He says His house shall be called a house of prayer." His house is a house of prayer. In that house, the blind and the lame came to Him and He healed them. If it's a house of prayer, it'll also be a house of healing and deliverance.

So if people say, "Oh, this is a house of prayer," but there is no manifest healing or deliverance, then you should question if it is truly a house of prayer. It may be a house of something. It may be a social club, a place where they gather together and play bingo, but it's not a house of prayer. Because if it were a house of prayer, you would see healing and you would see needs getting met for people who are hurting or oppressed. Only the Church of Jesus Christ can minister these graces, and only when both prayer and power are there.

Prayer and power are more important than having some famous healer in your midst. Even when you don't expect Him to, God will move in power in a true house of prayer. Some months ago, we were in Atlanta and I (Mahesh) had just finished ministering when I saw an elderly woman waving her hand to get my attention. She said, "Pastor, I can see."

I said, "God bless you, honey." (I thought she just saw my gestures.)

She was insistent, "Pastor I can *see.*"

I said, "That's wonderful." She just looked like an ordinary elderly person.

And then her helper said, "Pastor, Sister Alberta is 89 years old. She was born blind. She can see you right now. God has opened her eyes."

Whoa! Healing is still happening in God's house, wherever a place has been dedicated to Him in prayer.

In the house of prayer, you will be like the brave 5-year-old. You will tell the devil, "You can't do that in my house. Get out of my house." Men and women are waiting desperately for people who will come with the mantle of that authority and power. God does not want His house of prayer to be full of fear, but filled with men and women who will say, "Devil, get out of my house! Devil, get out of my city!"

God says, "I have an army of the angels of heaven that are about to be loosed that have not been loosed, but I want them to be loosed now through My sons and my daughters." Even when you find yourself in perilous situations, He has destined you to exercise His power and come through in victory. You will be the right person at the right time in the right place, with an army of angels that are going to be loosed, that are around you. You don't have to fear, because God does not give you a spirit of fear, but rather of power, of love, and of a sound mind (see 2 Tim. 1:7).

In 2008 we were holding one of our first watch services at our satellite church in a suburb just south of the downtown Atlanta area. As the watchmen began to worship and harmonize in prayer, one of the themes the Lord began to highlight for them was the airwaves and media outlets that had "exalted themselves against the knowledge of God" (see 2 Cor. 10:5). The watchmen began to declare from the book of Daniel *"You have been weighed in the balances, and found wanting"* (Daniel 5:27). They culminated with the prayer" You are Lord over this nation. Lord, we ask that You would reveal Yourself to the media that have exalted themselves and are promoting antichrist agendas. May those kingdoms bow to the Kingdom of the Lord Christ Jesus."

At about that time, one of the watchmen passed a note to The Watch captain saying, "We are under a tornado warning." The watchmen then turned their attention to pray for the safety of the people of Atlanta and protection from the storm.

As the watchmen were praying, a tornado tore through downtown Atlanta, striking the CNN tower, damaging much of the façade of the building as well as the newsroom. Yet, in the building next door, an SEC basketball tournament was in overtime, ensuring that fans were safe in the building rather than pouring out into the streets as the powerful tornado sent shards of glass and steal through the city. Amazingly, even though tens of thousands of people were in the direct path of the tornado, no one was killed in the storm that night, and most injuries were minor cuts and bruises.

We could see God's hand of protection—and His speedy response to our prayers concerning the media.

THE POWER OF MIDNIGHT PRAYER

The psalmist writes: *"At midnight I will rise to give thanks to You, because of Your righteous judgments"* (Ps. 119:62). This prayer of David was the cry of his watchman heart. The tradition of the descendants of King David is a tradition of keeping the watch, of wakefulness when the world is asleep in order to watch for and pray in God's righteousness.

Just as the exodus from Egypt began at midnight, there is a recurring history of redemption breaking in on God's people during the night. In the beginning, the Spirit of God brooded over the darkness and chaos; God spoke and there was light.

This is the pure essence of prayer. Prayer is intervention. Prayer is deliverance. Prayer is restoration. Prayer is breakthrough. Prayer is light! Gentile Christians ask one another, "Where do you go to church?" But the Jew asks, "Where do you pray?" The watchman tradition of King David still goes on today among the Hassids, the "charismatic" sect of Judaism. For them the watchman and the midnight hour are intrinsically linked to the final redemption of Israel. That redemption is vitally linked to the rebuilding of God's house of prayer for all nations, the Temple. *Tikkun Chatzot*, the midnight prayer, is a time of opportunity to recreate the world through watching in prayer.

It was the custom of Jesus and it was also the regular form of prayer for the earliest Christians to carry on the tradition of David's midnight watch. It is called "breaking the night," because the watchmen awaken to pray at the division point of the night, as one day ends and a new day begins. It is *mid*-night prayer. It follows the pattern of creation as "the evening and the morning were the first day." In a spiritual sense "the midnight hour" has the power of redemption. We have experienced this power of watching in prayer again and again personally as we have kept The Watch corporately every week for more than fourteen years at the writing of this book.

The word *chatzot* means "to cut into two." One of the main purposes of midnight prayer for the Jews is praying for the rebuilding of the temple, God's "house of prayer," as the place at the center of the world where His family can re-gather to enjoy the promise of His salvation.

In this tradition the watchman breaks his sleep in order to heed the cry of the Shekinah over the exile of God's people from Him and from their inheritance. This "bitter shriek" is muffled by the voice of the world. But in the midnight hours while the world sleeps the watchman, heeding the cry of the glory, rebuilds the walls of God's house of prayer.

The Power of the Midnight Watch

Watching in prayer has a two-fold nature of seemingly opposite elements. It is a dual cry: for the return of God's people to Him and for the return of God to His people. One folds into the other to form the power of prayers in the night watches. The watchman takes up the burden of the Lord for His people, for the sin that runs rampant, for the oppression suffered at the hands of the evil one and his messengers. This is true priestly ministry to which every believer has been called. We have been given "the ministry of reconciliation" that is of reconciling the world to God. Watching prayer provides the bookends for effective proclamation of the Gospel and breakthrough for miracles.

The history of breaking the night in prayer is a dramatic one. God cut covenant with Abraham in the night watch (see Gen. 15:5). That midnight travail, incidentally, was the moment in time that Israel's future redemption from Egypt was established. And when the deliverance of Passover came, it came at midnight (see Exod. 12:29). God promised Abraham and Sarah their heir in the night watch. "And He brought him outside and said, "Look toward the stars" (see Gen. 15:5). God delivered Sarah from the harem of a pagan king in the night watch (see Gen. 20:3). The angels came to deliver Lot in the first watch of the night (see Gen. 19:1). God met Jacob in the night watch—twice, once as he was going out of his inheritance with nothing but the clothes on his back and a stone for a pillow and again when he was coming to his inheritance possessing the double (see Gen. 28:11-16). Daniel broke through in prayers to God, communed with angel messengers, and changed the history of the world through his prayers and watching (see, for example, Dan. 7:13). It was in the night that God delivered Mordecai from Haman's plan to murder (see Esther 6). These are but a sampling of the power of breaking the night by watching in prayer.

Watching in prayer carries a "one-two punch" like no other. Not only does God bring deliverance and redemption to His people in the night watches, He also wreaks havoc on His enemies at the same time. *"So Pharaoh rose in the night, he, all his servants, and all the Egyptians; and there was a great cry in Egypt, for there*

192

was not a house where there was not one dead." (Exod. 12:30). Abimelech, Laban, Sennacherib, Nebuchadnezzar are just a few of the pagan rulers or enemies of Israel whose plans were destroyed or hearts were changed during the night.

There is also a sweet side to the hour of prayer made in the night watch. *Tikkun Chatzot* has the power of redemption. It sweetens harsh decrees."[1] One of the main prayers of Jews since the destruction of the temple is that God would rebuild it. The kingship of David was a prophetic announcement about the return of the reign of God over His people. The Talmud says: "A harp was hung above David's bed, and at the mid-point of the night a north wind would come and blow on it, and the harp would play by itself. He would get up at once and engage in Torah study and song until dawn."[2]

The night watches are a time of favor and repair, when Heaven is open and earth is ready to receive her King. As we arise in the night watches, we draw Heaven down and impose her statutes on earth which was created to reflect her atmosphere as the dwelling place of God walking in the midst of His family. It is an hour when the heavenly Bridegroom is knocking at her door: *"...Open to Me, My sister, My darling, My dove, My perfect one! For My head is drenched with dew, My locks with the damp of the night"* (Song of Sol. 5:2 NASB).

On this side of midnight, as the promise of day dawns, our hearts awaken as the earth awakens after the night. If you have ever spent the night out in the woods you know that morning comes very early and even before the first hint of daylight, birds begin to sing and call to one another. The travail of prayer that begins in watching is the first stanza in a psalm that ends with joy and praise of reunion with God.

God responds to our cry and comes to the hearts of His people to find His resting place there. This is the whole purpose of creation! This is the great accomplishment of His plan of redemption wrought in Christ. "Redemption will begin at *Chatzot*. And it will come about in the merit of those who get up for *Chatzot*."[3]

The Shulamite in the Song of Solomon is a prophetic vision of the Church. She says, *"I was asleep but my heart was awake"* when she hears a Voice (Song of Sol. 5:2). It is the voice of her Beloved calling her to watch with Him. At first she reasons: "I have taken off my dress…I have washed my feet…if I get up I have to dress, when I come back to bed I'll have to wash my feet again…" (see verse 3). There are always many excuses not to get up with Jesus. Usually many of those reasons are very practical. We have to sleep sometime or our minds and bodies break down. We have to go to work and provide for our families. We have to get the kids off to school or get to school ourselves. We have to make breakfast and keep our appointments for our business affairs, family, and friends.

But watching in prayer is like developing muscular strength. You can hardly believe you can keep regular times of going without sleep for the sake of communion with God until you do it. And once you establish a pattern of it in your life, you wonder how you ever got along without it! These are also the reasons why setting aside a particular time to watch during your week is very practical. We can arrange it into our schedule without letting regular responsibilities be neglected. Years ago for our Watch of the Lord, we chose Friday night. We call it "date night with Jesus." And that's what we do. We "go about the city, seeking Him whom [our] soul loves" just as the Shulamite searched for her lover.

In the tradition of *Tikkun Chatzot*, cutting the night in two with prayers and song, a Jew's "main devotion is to get up for Chatzot (mid-night prayer)"[4] Keeping the watch with His friends was one of the primary features of Jesus' prayer life. Praying alone and with His friends in the night watches was what made Him different in His ministry during the daytime. It was in the night watch where He picked up the vibration of Heaven. The night watch was where He went to refresh Himself and realign Himself with the Father's good pleasure, day-to-day.

The night watch was where Jesus stayed in harmony with Heaven while He was on earth.

ENDNOTES

1. *Likutey Moharan I,*149

2. *Berakhot* 3b.

3. Reb Noson of Breslov, *Likutey Halakhot, Hashkamat HaBoker* 1:15.

4. *Rabbi Nachman's Wisdom* #301.

CHAPTER 11

Ablaze in Beauty

...And the Glory Forever

RECOVERING TWO KEYS TO THE RETURN OF THE GLORY—HUMILITY AND THANKSGIVING.

Have you ever had one of those "flying dreams"? First, there's the sensation of trying to lift yourself up above an invisible gravity line. You can feel your body weight and your efforts seem clumsy and futile. You can't quite "get it" and you might crash. But like a boy learning to swim in a lake, there is ease in the glory once you rise to a certain level. After that it just "comes naturally." You are aloft, soaring! It is the most exhilarating thing in the world—flying without anything to keep you aloft but your heart.

Being a watchman in prayer can be like that at times. Our friend Ruth Heflin was a pioneer in the glory, and she was famous for her heart of worship. Her philosophy about "flying" in prayer was connected to what happens when Christians pray and sing. She used to say, "Praise until worship comes, worship until glory comes and then stay in the glory."

God expects us to arise and become intercessors—not to stay down, but to arise! We rise higher each time we gather to watch and pray. *"Arise, cry out in the night, at the beginning of the watches; pour out your heart like water before the face of the Lord. Lift your hands toward Him..."* (Lam. 2:19).

Arise! Cry out! God comes when He is invited. He is not looking for great ability, great anointing...but He is looking for people who are hungry for His presence. It is our duty to create an atmosphere of expectancy, to exercise the level of faith we presently possess, and to press in for His glory.

THANKFULNESS, HOPE, JOY

In staying awake to pray together, there is thankfulness, hope, and joy. Watchmen watch because they are expectantly looking toward the breaking light. Though it may be night, they know that the dawn is coming. This is the beauty of watching prayer. Psalms 119:62 says, *"At midnight I will rise to give thanks to You, because of Your righteous judgments."*

When it is darkest, what is our response? To get up and give thanks! At the midpoint between settings and risings we look not at the darkness around us, but we begin to seed the heavens with light. Psalms 22:3 tells us that the Lord is "enthroned on our praises." We break the darkness of the night with our praises, preparing a landing strip for the favor, blessings, and intervention of God's Kingdom to come down. We watch and pray in earnest expectation that the Lord is good and that He is the rewarder of those who earnestly seek Him.

In a time of great sorrow and wickedness, the psalmist wrote, *"When I thought how to understand this, it was too painful for me—until I went into the sanctuary of God; then I understood their end"* (Ps. 73:16-17). We go through seasons of midnight as churches, as nations, and as individuals, in many ways. Darkness will try to discourage and dissuade us from our authority and call. The greatest antidote for this discouragement, the best way to break the night, is to step into His presence, where we can see once again the events and circumstances unfolding on the earth from the heavenly vantage point of victory.

Thanksgiving is the key to opening our hearts and eyes to see and declare this victory as we become conscious of His awesome presence. Psalms 95:2 says, *"Let us come before His presence with thanksgiving; let us shout joyfully to Him with psalms."* Thanksgiving ushers us into His glorious presence. If we will spend time thanking instead of complaining, we'll find ourselves in the right frame of mind to enter His presence. Thanksgiving honors God for what He has done; praise honors who He is; and both will take us into what we like to call "presence prayer," prayer that is fueled by a distinct consciousness of the One to whom we pray.

Thanksgiving is often a choice, especially when the darkness seems to be overwhelming. Leviticus 22:29 says, *"And when you offer a sacrifice of thanksgiving to the Lord, offer it of your own free will."* Rising up in thanks may go against everything you feel and see, but this is what God instructs you to do. If you ever want to know the will of God in a situation, begin with praise. Give thanks even in your darkest hour. Your heavenly Father commands it. It's always in His will. Every fiber of your human nature may seem to be saying, "I don't want to; I don't want to! No, I don't feel like it." And yet if you will give the sacrifice of thanksgiving, that will be the key for things to turn around.

> *Let the peoples praise You, O God; let all the peoples praise You. Then the earth shall yield her increase; God, our own God, shall bless us* (Psalms 67:5-6).

Barren wilderness seasons in our lives, in our churches, and our nation provide us with perfect opportunities to rise up in praise to the Lord. Thanksgiving opens the heavens and causes the earth to yield her increase. Give thanks and praise, and the harvest will come.

Are we looking only for relief, for answers to our need? No, we are looking to the One who holds the universe. Our destination is the throne of God, the presence of God. Our guarantee that we will arrive at our destination is the sound of thanks and praise, the joyful noise comes out of our mouths as if we have already arrived—which in a way we have.

The priests ministering in the temple would daily go before the altar to watch—to lift up prayer and incense before the mercy seat of the Lord. Jesus is our ultimate watchman, the One who plumbed the depths of the grave and the wrath due all mankind in joyful expectation of the goodness and mercy that would be extended to all who would believe in the finished work of His blood sprinkled on the mercy seat on our behalf.

He has invited His Body on the earth, the watching and praying Church, to arise in the night to sing praises to Him, enter His presence and extend His Kingdom into the dark regions of the earth all around us. In His presence is the anointing that breaks the yoke. As we access His presence in praise and thanksgiving in the midnight hour, it is like activating the electricity to turn on the lights in a darkened room. In the same way, when you give thanks, you are turning on the switch for the power of God to flow through you. Thanksgiving is the switch for the glory of the Lord to arise upon the Church in the darkness of night.

ASCENDING TO GLORY

The oldest, fixed daily prayer in Judaism is the *Shema*. This consists of Deuteronomy 6:4-9, Deuteronomy 11:13-21, and Numbers 15:37-41 and it can be summarized follows:

Deuteronomy 6:4-9—"Hear O Israel! The Lord is our God, the Lord alone. You shall love the Lord your God with all your heart and with all your soul and with all your might...."

Deuteronomy 11:13-21—"...Obey My words that He might grant rain and impress, imprint, press into your heart these words of Mine that you might dwell in the land as long as there is a Heaven...."

Numbers 15:37-41—"Observe all My commandments and be holy for your God."

The first paragraph includes a command to speak of these matters "when you retire and when you arise." From ancient times, this commandment was fulfilled by reciting the Shema twice a day, morning and night. The whole congregation of Israel still rises each morning and retires each night with the words of the Shema. It's the spinal column of Jewish prayer according to the revelation of Moses when he asked, "Lord, show me Your glory."

When Moses made this monumental request, God said, *"I will make all My goodness pass before you, and I will proclaim the name of the Lord before you"* (Exod. 33:19). And God passed before Moses, having placed him in a cleft of the rock and covered him with His hand. God called out, declaring His name as He went.

When God declared His name, it was not a pronouncement like a rodeo announcer naming the next contestant. When God declared His name, Moses experienced God's presence and was permeated with a revelation of who God is. It was more than just an audible word; it was a spiritual experience, a mind, body, and spirit "knowing."

Thus Moses' face shone like the sun for days afterward because he had been permeated with the Presence. God's presence had flash-fried Moses on a cellular level. This one-time event on

Sinai helps us grasp the fullness we can experience today in Christ Jesus.

Here's what the Jewish sages think happened next[1]:As the Lord passed before Moses, the Holy One wrapped Himself in a *tallit*, or a prayer shawl, like a *shaliach tzibbur* (prayer leader), and showed Moses the order of prayer. He said to him, "Whenever Israel sins, let them perform this order before Me, and I shall forgive them." Moses had asked to apprehend the truth of God's existence in a distinct manner. In response to Moses' request, God enwrapped Himself, as it were—showing that mortal man cannot completely grasp His reality: *"You shall see My back: but My face shall not be seen"* (Exod. 33:23). But there was a sense of complete presence; it was clear that behind the tallit covering, there was something great and mighty.

Shema, the Lord Is One

The entire Jewish prayer liturgy, the *siddur* or "order," comes from this event. Rising up early in the morning and praying the Shema, faithful Jews count 13 attributes of God's mercy revealed: compassion before man sins; compassion after man has sinned; compassion to give all creatures according to their need; mercy; graciousness; slowness to anger; plenteousness in mercy; complete truth; keeping mercy to a thousand generations; forgiving iniquity; forgiving transgression; forgiving sin; and pardoning.

Having recited these attributes to remind themselves of the fullness of God's glory they say: "And now, the strength of God shall increase." In Judaism, the attributes of God are not theology. They are revelations, manifestations of God's presence in the world. But God does not impose His presence on the world. God is found where people, created in the image of God, call on His name. Every day, at every prayer, Jews declare: *"Yitgadel ve-yitkadesh shemei raba"*— "His great name shall be sanctified and increased!"

Why have we given you all this information about Moses and Jewish liturgy? To show that Jesus *is* the Shema, the divine anthropomorphosis of the answer to Moses' prayer at last! Christ Himself is the Shema which God declared that day on the mountain. As the *chazzan* (prayer leader) He recreated the scene with Moses on the mountain when He was transfigured before the disciples. And as their prayer leader, He fulfilled the ages of Jewish prayers in the Shema when He prayed:

> *"That they all may be one, as You, Father, are in Me, and I in You; that they also may be one in Us, that the world may believe that You sent Me. And the glory which You gave Me I have given them, that they may be one just as We are one: I in them, and You in Me; that they may be made perfect in one, and that the world may know that You have sent Me, and have loved them as You have loved Me.*
>
> *"Father, I desire that they also whom You gave Me may be with Me where I am, that they may behold My glory which You have given Me; for You loved Me before the foundation of the world"* (John 17:21-24).

...that we may be One together in Him: "Shema, Israel!" God is One.

From Glory to Glory

There are two further important points to note. One is glory *(Shekinah)* and one is joy.

The glory of God is the majesty of the fullness of His Person, unchanging, perfect, and eternal. The mystery of this perfection is that He loves us, has created us, and has revealed Himself to us. By clothing Himself in the flesh like the man He made, He has fulfilled His desire to be intimately reunited in an eternal bond, a covenant more intricate and complete than marriage between a man and a woman, an encompassing intimacy of bliss, which will not be broken again. God humbled Himself in Christ and was born of a virgin. Christ humbled Himself as a man, the Son, and became obedient unto death that He might purchase for the Father the one gift God craved—us. He has humbled Himself again as He has poured Himself out of the throne to which He was restored after His resurrection, pouring Himself into our bodies by His Spirit!

The glory, who passed before Moses on Sinai, who traveled in the pillar with Israel in the wilderness, who rested over the ark in the tabernacle, who entered through the doors of the temple as Solomon sanctified it, whom Ezekiel saw at the River Chebar, who marched before John by the Jordan, who was transfigured before the disciples, has come home to rest in each person who receives Christ.

The Shekinah is no longer in exile.

This is the progression from glory to glory, beginning thousands of years ago on Sinai. We are in the final phase of that progression. There shall be one more revealing, and it shall be the last. We shall be like Him when He appears in glory.

Then the fulfillment of Moses' prayer and the prayer of Jesus in John 17 will come. We shall be one in Him as He is One. This is the answer to Jesus' high priestly prayer for us. This is the "at-one-ment" wrought in His blood.

How it boggles the mind to realize that God has been working, since He spoke light into the chaos at the beginning, to come to this day for Himself. The travail of the earth and Israel's birth pangs, the cries of the prophets and the incense of the priests, the blood of the Cross and the fire of Pentecost—all for this: that we might be one in Him with the Father. From glory to glory. The prayers we pray have their eschaton: His appearing from Heaven to claim those who are His own.

We are not afraid because of the darkness. We are neither frightened by antichrists nor beasts nor wicked men who do not repent. The love of God has delivered us from fear in this world. Our faces look for the dawn. We continue in unceasing fellowship, watching in prayer and allowing Him to reveal Himself through our hearts and our faces.

Glory Cloud

From time to time, watchmen experience God's tangible presence. Sometimes it looks like a cloud. Always it is awe-inspiring. Perhaps your own experience parallels what was related by some of our watchmen:

> Back at the very beginning of last year, during The Watch, I had an incredible vision. At that point, I was fresh out of my old life and knew nothing of the signs, wonders, miracles, and manifestations of the Spirit that we see in our corporate body. During The Watch on this particular night, Pastor Bonnie indicated that there was "…an incredible spirit of prophecy here." Prophetic words were being given in such great numbers that I was utterly amazed. I thought to myself that it was like they were receiving instant downloads and then giving the words to the intended recipients.
>
> At that moment, my eyes were opened in the Spirit. I saw a white but fierce cloud swirling around the perimeter of the ceiling. I had never seen or heard of anything like that in my life. I had absolutely no idea what I was seeing. I saw what appeared to be static discharges coming from the swirling cloud and "zapping" people in the head. Those people were instantly given words for people. There were brilliant flashes of white within this cloud.
>
> I was so overwhelmed that I ran out of the building, saying to myself, "I've got to call someone…I've got to call someone." My mother is a Spirit-filled, prayer-and-fasting

warrior, so I called her and told her what I had seen. I didn't mention this to anyone else for fear of being seen as "flaky." Eventually I told someone I trusted, and she smiled and excitedly said, "That was the glory cloud." That was the coolest thing I had ever seen.

Another watchman recounts:

In 1996, the Lord visited us during the early morning hours of The Watch with a supernatural breeze from Heaven that "kissed" the watchmen, overwhelming our senses with lovely smells and sounds from Heaven. We wept and laughed and bowed down in adoration as Jesus swept through our midst over and over again. It was the first time that I was a part of an entire group of people having the same heavenly experience corporately, and it confirmed my decision to spend every Friday night at the feet of my Kinsman-Redeemer.

Learning to Rest and to War at the Same Time

We believe that every Christian is called to be a watchman. It is more than just praying prayers. It's more than just being a private or individual intercessor. It's a prophetic experience and a real entering into the identity of both the Bride and the army which are just part of the expression of the Church. The Watch gives place and opportunity for a corporate experience of that bridal intimacy of hearing the voice of the Lord, responding to Him, awakening the Lord to move on behalf of the Church, on behalf of our families, our children, our nations.

The Watch is also the advancing battalion of warriors releasing the promises and declarations of the Word of the Lord, hearing prophetically through dreams and visions, and literally standing in the broken-down gap to build up the wall and advance the Kingdom. The Watch is a time of unmatched intimacy, but it is also the time that we go to war. The more the merrier! There is strength in numbers.

One of our watchmen had a vision one night of herself as a beautiful bride. She recognized the Bride of Christ, adorned in the splendor of her full wedding raiment. As she admired her beauty, she looked down and discovered that this bride was wearing combat boots! This is a fitting illustration of the Body of Christ and our dual identity as a warrior bride.

Another intercessor who watches with us in Charlotte shared:

I have been coming to The Watch now for ten years. Here's how I got called to be a watchman.

I was awakened in the middle of the night by a very loud trumpet blast in my ear and I sat straight up to attention and I heard the audible voice of God for the first time in my life and He said, "Get your boots on. You're in My army now." I had a picture of myself in a wedding dress with black combat boots on and I knew that I was called to this church called All Nations Church even though I'd never been to it.

I showed up that first Friday night, which was a Watch service. When I walked in, the Holy Spirit said, "You're home now." I knew that I was called to this thing called The Watch. I didn't even know really what intercession was. I was new to a lot of this type of thing, but I knew that I had been called to something, to take my place on the wall. I've been here ever since.

The end of Psalm 23 in The Message version of the Bible reads like this: *"Your beauty and love chase after me every day of my life. I'm back home in the house of God for the rest of my life"* (Ps. 23:6 TM).

There is a Sabbath rest in keeping the watch that is supernatural. We labor to enter His rest as we give ourselves to fasting from sleep and attending to God's agendas in the corporate watch. That deep peace and restful confidence come not only into our individual lives, but also to our households, our churches, our cities.

Prayer is meant to further the effects of "resting" in the Lord. While it is serious business and is costly, if it becomes an onerous yoke of labor, it is not true, Spirit-inbreathed prayer. The prophet Jeremiah had a long vision in the night. At the end, the Lord summed it up:

> *Thus says the Lord of hosts, the God of Israel: "They shall again use this speech in the land of Judah and in its cities, when I bring back their captivity: 'The Lord bless you, O home of justice, and mountain of holiness!' And there shall dwell in Judah itself, and in all its cities together, farmers and those going out with flocks. For I have satiated the weary soul, and I have replenished every sorrowful soul."*
>
> *After this I awoke and looked around, and my sleep was sweet to me* (Jeremiah 31:23-26).

ASCENDING IN PRAYER

To reach new heights of glory as we learn to both rest and war, we need to ascend to God as David did in his psalms. There are fifteen songs of "ascent" or "going up" in the prayers of David in the Bible. These psalms, numbers 120 through 134, are the "building" songs. They correspond to the steps that were in the temple upon which the Levites would ascend with their instruments, chanting David's words. With each step they came nearer the great doors that opened into the sanctuary where the Shekinah rested over the ark as the testimony of God's presence in the midst of His people.

With each physical step, the priests took with them words of the prayers their King David had penned during the night watches, as the wind had strummed the strings of his harp and awakened the strings of his heart.

At every new level, the worshipers also ascended higher and higher into the ecstasy and joy of communion with God. They were ascending spiritually into Heaven as they approached the doors of His temple. At the same time their prayers were building—building up their hearts, building up their faith, building up Israel, building up Jerusalem, building up the temple.

As we watch together in prayer, we enter the realms of communion with God where the veil between Heaven and earth grows exceedingly thin. We reach places of revelation; we see both the spiritual realm and the earthly realms more clearly. It is no accident that we can see more clearly as the result of "watching"—with our eyes and our hearts open.

The fifteen songs of ascent begin with the cry of a man in trouble—surrounded by enemies, under threat of war, and in turmoil because he longs for a place of peace. This is where watching begins. We see the world in turmoil, we find our hearts in need of correction and restoration, we travail for lost loved ones, promises failed, plans gone awry. But where do we turn? We look *up*.

At first we might think that there is something we can do, someone we can get help from, something out there in this world that is just beyond reach but when we lay hold of it all will be well. But as we awake in our hearts, we come to know that there is no one who can help us but God Himself. As we watch with Him, we begin to know that He never sleeps and is always thinking of us.

That assurance begins to replace our unsettled feelings. We are changed. Our perspective and our priorities change. Our crises are calmed. We begin to rise in faith, in awareness of God, in knowledge of His will and assurance of His promise.

The psalms of ascent are the psalms that the Hebrew people sang whenever they journeyed up to Jerusalem for feasts and festivals. Starting out from their homes and towns, they met up on the roads leading from every direction to Jerusalem and they all sang these psalms together. When they reached their destination, they sang once more from Psalms 120 through 134:

○ Psalm 120: This is the condition we find ourselves in. We acknowledge our need and pour out our prayers.

○ Psalm 121: We realize our answer won't come from this realm. Our watching God is our "shield" and we recognize that we need His help. God says, "I AM everything you need. Trust in Me. Cling to Me. Believe Me. Ask Me. Expect Me to act."

○ Psalm 122: Joy comes from experiencing His presence in the midst of His people. We long for His judgments because they set the world right.

○ Psalm 123: We draw near to God as we adjust our priorities and prejudices, opinions and alliances to line up with His.

○ Psalm 124: Our vision has been lifted. Before, we saw only trouble around us; now we see God as King over all. We begin to draw the heavenly Kingdom into earth.

○ Psalm 125: We trust in the Lord and place our confidence in the fruit of righteousness in spite of the wicked.

○ Psalm 126: The joy of the Lord is our strength. There is no greater wealth than contentment. We rejoice because we have wept precious tears of travail and we rejoice in advance, expecting a great harvest.

○ Psalm 127: The secret place of the watchman is the resting place of trust. It is He who works mightily in us and not we of our own strength. God builds His house as we rest and watch with Him.

○ Psalm 128: The fear of the Lord brings blessing from Zion that breaks out beyond ourselves and blesses future generations.

○ Psalm 129: We have been delivered by God's faithfulness. We are soaring free from the reach of the wicked who might accuse or seek to destroy.

○ Psalm 130: We watch for the Lord like watchmen who wait for the morning sun. Expectation for Him draws us up out of the depths of despair and darkness into the brightness of His glory.

○ Psalm 131: Humility clothes us. We are content and secure. Even in times of uncertainty, there is wisdom in silent, patient dependence on God's greatness.

○ Psalm 132: We refuse spiritual sleep until He comes in fullness and takes up His abode. There He will be surrounded by His anointed ones in the fulfillment of the ancient promise.

○ Psalm 133: At last we have come to perfection, in harmony and unity and everlasting life.

○ Psalm 134: We have reached the height at last and stand there together, hands raised, faces up. In unity we cry "Holy!"

The themes of humility and thanksgiving echo as the priests go up in these fifteen steps of ascending into the glory. They remind us of future promises of Heaven. They refresh us and fill our hearts with the oil of the Spirit so that we can faithfully keep our charge of prayer and service in the purest form.

Like a Ladder

The way up in the Kingdom of God is always down. There is no story of glory that is not the story of humility.

Jacob laid hold of his inheritance in a seemingly under-handed way. But he learned obedience through the things he suffered on his journey back to success and greatness. So did Joseph. Even Jesus came down, making Himself low for our sakes, before He ascended to His throne for eternity.

As Jacob fled after he had tricked Esau out of the rights of the firstborn, he spent his first night in the wilderness with a stone for a pillow. At this low point he cried out to God, asking for His presence to go with him and vowing to honor God before all in return. During the night he dreamed a spiritual dream. In it, a portal was opened between Heaven and earth, and on a ladder angels carried things into Heaven and brought things back down.

This speaks to us of our own sojourning in prayer. We can only experience Heaven to the degree we experience Jesus. He is our open door, our portal by which we enter God's presence. As we are "in Him" and He is in Heaven, we also are transported by the Spirit to spiritual heights. But the way up is down.

During the writing of this book, which is about the practicality of living life on God's ladder of glory through watching prayer, I (Bonnie) dreamed a very strange dream. In it, I lived on a ladder that stretched over the walls of my house. On the ladder, I managed with some skill to step from rung to rung, moving about with pots and pans preparing food for my household. Every once in a while a member of my family or a friend from church came into the house below and would stand there asking me to look from my elevated vantage point to tell them where something they sought could be found or if another person was in a different part of the house and how to get there from where they stood.

It was not completely comfortable to live up there on that ladder. I felt quite self-conscious as people looked up to where I was. They didn't take my position as something particularly unusual or seem aware that it was inconvenient to live and serve from up there. The other people in the dream just seemed to accept my help from the ladder.

Upon waking, I reflected on the dream and realized it was a parable for watching in prayer. The words from Proverbs 31 came alive. That chapter personifies the Church as a virtuous wife. She prepares food for her household and brings goods from afar. She strengthens herself for the work and makes sure that her lamp does not go out during the night.

So it is with the Bride of Jesus who is constantly filled with His Spirit. We are living on the ladder stretching between the will of God in Heaven and His Kingdom advancing on earth. As we watch with Him in prayer, all the members of our household benefit. It is our "reasonable service" just as Christ considered it His reasonable service as the Son of the Father to make intercession for us.

From the beginning, prayer was a corporate work. Father, Son, and Spirit were joined together as one in one purpose: the salvation of the world. We enter into unity with that work as we awaken our hearts to watch in prayer. The very first word of Jesus' model prayer is "our"—us together—meaning prayer is a corporate experience.

As the community of God prays, He builds His house. "My house is called a house of prayer." As His tabernacle is raised up, the Shekinah, the glory of His manifest presence, has a place to which it can return.

Where the glory resides, darkness is overwhelmed with light. This is what John meant when he testified that *"We saw the glory with our own eyes, the one-of-a-kind glory....The Life-Light blazed out of the darkness; the darkness couldn't put it out"* (John 1:14,5 TM).

Jacob's vision was of the future temple, filled with glory, innumerable angels assisting a great company of priests as they went about in the house of the Lord, fulfilling their ministry—offering sacrifices, making intercession, and lifting up praises to God.

ENDNOTE

1. This is the description widely used by Jewish sages when describing the events on Sinai in the context of teaching on prayer.

CHAPTER 12

Yes! Yes! Yes!

...Amen!

THE "SO BE IT" OF WATCH PRAYER IS JESUS. HE IS OUR "AMEN"!

The Amazon rainforest has long been recognized as an important source of the world's rainwater. The sheer mass of trees makes this great forest like the lungs of the world. The leafy canopy catches rainwater as it falls and keeps it easily available to the atmosphere when the sun comes out again. What rain reaches the forest floor is taken up by the roots of the trees and then comes up to be drawn back out into the atmosphere. When the sun shines on the jungle canopy, millions of gallons of water are released as water vapor. In a matter of hours, the clear sky will begin to form clouds and rain showers will begin to fall again. This process happens much faster here than in any other environment. Researchers can watch storms that would take days and weeks to form in other regions literally develop before their eyes in a matter of hours on a daily basis in the rain forest. The rains that form over the Amazon serve as a reservoir of water that travels on the trade winds from South America across to Africa, serving to water the globe.

The praying, corporate Church, awakened and undulating with the rhythms of the Spirit of prayer, creates a spiritual canopy for revival and visitation to come upon the thirsty earth. This lush atmosphere of the presence of God teems with possibility for renewal, growth, and an ever-increasing cycle of life, as prayers ascend to God and return as He visits His people. We become the "lungs" for the world, breathing in and breathing out, inhaling the presence of God and exhaling His will in the earth.

Isaiah 61:3 declares that those on whom the Spirit rests will be called, *"trees of righteousness, the planting of the Lord that He may be glorified."* The prayers of the Church, multiplied by the corporate gathering, transform and affect the atmosphere not just locally, but globally. Our prayers are life to the world, sending the rains of Heaven across the nations. Corporate watching prayer is vital to the spiritual health and prosperity and harvest of the nations. James 5:7 says, *"So be patient, brethren, [as you wait] till the coming of the Lord. See how the farmer waits expectantly for the precious harvest from the land. [See how] he keeps up his patient [vigil] over it until it receives the early and late rains"* (AMP). Let us not grow weary and faint, let us not give up the gathering together, but let us keep vigil, burning with the oil of the Spirit, that the rains of revival will come and water the earth with His glorious presence, and usher in His return and the ultimate establishment of His Kingdom.

ASK FOR THE RAIN!

A great force of God's power will be released as we commit ourselves to effective prayer. In Acts 4, we read how the Christians prayed together with one heart, mind, and spirit. Then all the believers were united as they lifted their voices in prayer (see

Acts 4:24). The result of that prayer was a great shaking and a fresh outpouring of God's grace and boldness to share the Gospel.

> *...The effective, fervent prayer of a righteous man avails much. Elijah was a man with a nature like ours, and he prayed earnestly that it would not rain; and it did not rain on the land for three years and six months. And he prayed again, and the heaven gave rain, and the earth produced its fruit* (James 5:16-18).

Haggai 2 speaks of a time when everything that can be shaken will be shaken, and then *"they shall come to the Desire of All Nations, and I will fill this temple with glory"* (Hag. 2:7).

The power of consistent, committed, corporate prayer cannot be underestimated in the advent of our returning King. Our prayers shake the earth and shift the atmosphere, seeding the heavens with revival rains to fall on the earth. *"Ask the Lord for rain in the time of the latter rain. The Lord will make flashing clouds; He will give them showers of rain, grass in the field for everyone"* (Zech. 10:1).

The Word Seeds the Clouds

There was a family that drove all the way from New Mexico to Texas where I (Mahesh) was pastoring at the time. They were desperate. They had five cute little kids, and the mother had terminal breast cancer. She was going to die pretty soon. Those little kids were hanging onto their mommy; they didn't realize that their mommy was going to die in a few weeks. The doctors had done all they could. She was comparatively a young woman, and just out of her twenties.

So I prayed for her. I did not feel one ounce of anointing, or grace, or anything, and yet I was desperate for her, desperate especially because of the kids. I went home feeling I had failed; I knew those kids were going to lose their mother.

221

That week they went to the Lubbock Methodist Hospital for some advanced tests and treatments, and they phoned our church to let us know that the doctors could not find one trace of the malignancy, that the whole cancer had gone away completely! I said, "How could this happen? I hadn't felt a thing, and had not thought a thing had happened."

Then the Lord showed me this Scripture:

> *Then they cried out to the Lord in their trouble, and He saved them out of their distresses He sent His word and healed them, and delivered them from their destructions* (Psalm 107:19-20).

The Lord said, "As you spoke over her, I sent My Word to heal her. This cancer was sent to destroy her, but I sent My Word." The Word is an agent, filled with the glory of God, which will destroy the agencies of destruction around us. The Word releases the glory of God to fall like healing, life-giving rain.

"The Word of God is alive and active and full of power" (see Hebrews 4:12). I had a vision once in which I saw a nail that had gone through the Word of God and it was bleeding. At that point, I realized that the Word is alive. The life is in the blood. That woman was healed because God sent His Word and healed her, and cancer could not stand in the anointed presence of the Word of God.

There is a level where we can pray the Word mechanically and repeat the Word in our effort to bring down God's power and see breakthrough. However, God is calling us to an intimate knowledge of Him in the glory. Jesus is the Living Word. He is the I AM who encompasses all we need or can ask. As we honor the Word as a living embodiment of the presence of Christ, seeing the glory in the Word, singing the Word, and speaking it out loud, the more it becomes the fully alive Word of God in our midst.

The Greek verb that means "to watch" is *gregoreuo*. I believe that it's no accident that Gregorian chants, a form of Scripture-based singing prayer named for Gregory the Great (590-604), have been releasing God's power for centuries through corporate songs praying the Word. Sung according to the Canonical Hours derived from the Jewish practice of reciting prayers at set times of the day, the sound of many voices rise as one like incense from the altar of prayer throughout the day and during the watches of the night.

There are different ways you can get in tune with the Lord. You can pray in tongues; you can enter into anointed worship; you can enter into the glory of the Word of God, speak it out loud, and release it through your proclamation.

God says He knows *"the end from the beginning, and from ancient times things that are not yet done, saying 'My counsel shall stand, and I will do all My pleasure'"* (Isa. 46:10). The Word of God frames our existence regardless of our current circumstances. When we get in tune with the Word of God the empty places in our lives are filled. The promises still waiting are released. The Word is alive and you can enter into it. What are the things that are in your life today that are empty? What are the promises that you are still waiting to see fulfilled? *Wait on the Lord in His Word.* Don't try to step in and "help" God in the flesh. In the time between the promise of the Word and fulfillment of His promise Abraham tried to help God and begot Ishmael. Elijah believed the Word of the Lord and positioned himself to watch and pray, his eyes set on the horizon in faith. He didn't waiver though the sky was clear and dry.

It is difficult to wait. That's why it's helpful to have the Body of Christ around you. It's helpful to have spiritual fathers and mothers who can say, "We are praying, we are praying, we are praying. Hold on." You don't have to settle for an Ishmael, God is going to give you Isaac.

One thing you don't need to fast from is the Word of God! Keep on receiving it and sending it out into the atmosphere and you will keep on receiving new strength. The Word of God builds you up and strengthens you. The Word of God sustains you in such a way that prevents you from backsliding, and guarantees your victory over sin.

The Word is there to shield you and to be used as a weapon of aggression against the enemy. When our son Ben was born, he had a terminal kidney condition. After an intense battle, our son was healed and God gave him new kidneys. However, every year after that there was an evil spirit that would come and try to make him sick on the anniversary of when he was first taken ill, and he would become deathly sick again. For several weeks, this spirit of death would linger. One time he got so sick that he could not keep any water down. Of course, he couldn't eat, and he was getting weaker and weaker. I (Mahesh) said, "Not again. I don't want to take him to the hospital again."

Suddenly the Word of God came, and God said, "Turn to Exodus 23:25." I didn't even know it existed in the Bible. The Word of the Lord said, "Speak this word over your son and let him speak it out." (By this time, our son was old enough to speak.) The passage was, *"So you shall serve the Lord your God, and He will bless your bread and your water. And I will take sickness away from the midst of you."*

And I said, "Ben, say this: "God is blessing my water and my bread." He said, "Daddy in pain, God…" and he was really getting weak. "…Jesus is blessing my water and my bread, and He's taking sickness away from my midst."

And the Holy Spirit came over him. He kind of closed his eyes for a moment, and you could see his color come back, and a few minutes later he said, "Daddy, I'm thirsty."

I gave him some soda, and then about an hour later I think, we gave him some crackers and he was able to keep them down, and the next day he woke up totally healed. The wonderful thing is that the shadow of death never came back again to hurt him again in that way, praise the Lord!

JOY IN THE MORNING

Prayer has traditionally been perceived by Christians as a necessary and even obligatory part of our relationship with God. What has been lacking in our perspective on prayer has been the *joy*, the *adventure*, the *power*, and the *privilege* of prayer. According to the Bible's own testimony, revelation is entirely the gracious self-disclosure of the utterly transcendent and otherwise hidden God in the person of Jesus Christ. Jesus, as Karl Barth has said, is "the divine Yes to man and his cosmos."[1]

> *Whatever God has promised gets stamped with the Yes of Jesus. In Him, this is what we preach and pray, the great Amen, God's Yes and our Yes together, gloriously evident. God affirms us, making us a sure thing in Christ, putting His Yes within us. By His Spirit He has stamped us with His eternal pledge—a sure beginning of what He is destined to complete (2 Corinthians 1:20-22 TM).*

> *He who did not spare His own Son, but delivered Him up for us all, how shall He not with Him also freely give us all things?* (Romans 8:32).

Joy is not to be confused with happiness. Happiness is related to physical pleasure and satiation of the demands of the mind and body. Pleasantness makes us happy. A surprise gift makes us happy. An unexpected visit from a loved one makes us happy. A garden full of flowers makes us happy. Happiness is not evil, but it is as unstable as a windsock which changes direction on the air current. Joy is different. Joy comes from a wellspring in subterranean depths of being that is impervious to the tremors of the topsoil of body and mind. Joy is spiritual. It is a gift from the Spirit to our spirit.

Christianity has been dour too long. The joy that Jesus had is too seldom mentioned and perhaps too little sought by those He has revealed Himself to. The psalmist sang Him this anthem: *"You love righteousness and hate wickedness; therefore God, Your God, has anointed You with the oil of gladness more than Your companions"* (Ps. 45:7). But in truth it seems that those who were most offended by wickedness have been the most sour. Or at least this is what we see in those few Pharisees who seemed to enjoy very little of what Jesus did and even less of who He was. The key to the joy Jesus had was His oneness with the Father. It meant that He was most joyful when His Father was most pleased. Are you like that? Have you considered that God has limited Himself to you? There are works and words of love and presence in the community where God has placed you through which God is yearning to play among His children. He seems to care to be out on display before those who have their backs turned. He wants to get their attention. The joy of Jesus was in complete self-sacrifice. This shows us the perfection of God. He has not changed. He is changing us! The joy of Heaven is the nature of self giving love.

Jesus meant it when He said, "I delight to do Your will." It was not a decision it was a proclamation that obedience thrilled him! Delight is not the same as happiness. Happiness is that state of human relief from our otherwise miserable state of discontent when we do not get our way. The mission of Jesus was to bring joy. Abraham rejoiced to see it. The angels rejoiced when they announced Him. Heaven thunders with this joy every time a sinner turns to Christ. John rejoiced in Elizabeth's womb. Anna and Simeon rejoiced when they saw Him in the temple. The multitudes rejoiced to see His miracles. Jesus rejoiced to see His disciples working miracles. All this joy is His and can be ours. There is little record of the possibility of perpetual human "happiness" as we have defined it in the lives of those first- and second-century Christians. Yet they were known, as their Master had been, for their joy. As Paul said in the context of persecution, shipwreck, stoning and facing down the beasts of the Roman circus: "Rejoice in the Lord always: and again I say, rejoice" (see Phil. 4:4).

Jesus is the divine Yes, the Alpha and the Omega, the first and the last. He breaks the seal on the Book of Life. He is the divine "Amen" ("so be it")! As The Message renders the "amen" of Jesus' model prayer in Matthew 6:13—*"Yes. Yes. Yes."* Simply put, the joy of the Lord, the highest delight possible, is the reunion of man with God.

In keeping the watch, we find this theme as we refer back to that vision of His feet as the feet of Boaz (see Chapter 1), our bridegroom in the day of harvest. The pomegranates and bells, which ringed the hem of the priests' garments and danced against their feet as they performed their prayers on this festival and others, are the symbols of this joy. We are not only uncovering His feet to awaken Him on our behalf, we are also crowning and anointing His head, as it were, with oil, making Him King. The anointing and crowning of a king is always accompanied by intense joy. Watching in prayer, we crown Him with joy, as He has said, "I will make them joyful in My house of prayer for all nations" (see Isa. 56:7).

As Jesus portrayed in His high priestly prayer "that they may be one, Father, as We are one, I in them and You in Me, that they may become perfectly one, so that the world may know that You sent me" (see John 17:21-23), that we may see His glory that He had in the beginning. The mission of Jesus: joy unspeakable and full of glory. Thus the joy of the angels, the shepherds, the mother of John and John in her womb, of Anna and Simeon, of all these watchmen who waited for His appearing and rejoiced to see His face.

Face-Up in Expectation

As we mentioned in the Introduction and in Chapter 3, the posture of prayer depicted in early Christian art, especially in the paintings and drawings that decorate the Roman catacombs, reflects the standard posture for prayer adopted by the first Christians. So prevalent is this posture that art historians called it "orant," from *orare*, the Latin verb "to pray." The orant figure, depicted with eyes and arms raised and palms extended toward Heaven, illustrates that the early Christians prayed with face-up expectation.

The ultimate end to our prayers is the return of Christ, which the whole world shall see together. With every prayer we pray there should be an undercurrent of watching and waiting for His return as the final answer to our prayers and the true fulfillment of our worship. The prayers of the watchman are awake with that promise and filled with the consolation and assurance His lasting triumph will bring. This is what makes them different from other ways of praying. The hidden power of watching in prayer returns us to our ancient roots of those first Christians who, in the midst of seasons of terrible opposition and persecution, advanced the Kingdom in power and joy as they stood with eyes open, arms raised, faces upturned and hearts ready to leap forward into the arms of the Lamb at His return. This expectancy pervaded their lives and was watered at the wells of their prayer. While we press through in prayers for intervention and miracles, for peace and security, for provision and deeper communion with God now, our true reward will come when we see Him face to face. The words you want to hear more than testimonies of what He has accomplished because of your prayers are the words of the Master, "Well done, good and faithful servant. Enter into the joy of your Lord!"

True prayer will lead us to watching. "We do not watch just because of the dangers that threaten us. We are expecting the salvation of the world. We are watching for God's advent. With tense attention, we open all our senses for the coming of God into our lives, into our society, to this earth."[2]

Until then, Christians have been called to take their place with Christ in prayer. From Heaven we are seated with Him in the mountain of the house of the Lord. Watching together we are face-up in prayer, no longer hiding from Him or from ourselves or from our place as watchmen around the wall of this city. Out of our caves and into His light, we are discovering and revealing the hidden power of watching and praying. Face-up in expectation, we are watching until he comes. Yes! Yes! Yes!

ENDNOTES

1. Karl Barth, *Church Dogmatics* IV.2, G.W. Bromiley, T.F. Torrance eds., (London: T. & T. Clark International, 2004), 180.

2. Jürgen Moltmann and Elisabeth Moltmann-Wendel, *Passion for God: Theology in Two Voices* (Louisville, KY: Westminster-John Knox Press, 2003), 62.

Epilogue

Go Set a Watch

How does one go about setting a watch and awakening to watching in prayer?

The first practical step is making a place. As the saying goes, "Location. Location. Location." Prepare a particular place where you regularly go to watch in prayer. It can be a room set aside in your home or apartment that is your special sanctuary for prayer and study. It can be the kitchen after the kids are off to school or the living room after dinner. It can be the back porch or the church sanctuary or Sunday school room. But have one place that has room for others beside yourself where you meet on a particular day at a particular time with regularity. If you keep The Watch in your home, find or develop some believers who love Jesus as much or more than you do and watch with them.

Then choose a regular time. In our church, we have chosen Friday night. It is the end of the week and so there is no worry about a morning work schedule for most. It is also a good way to enter the rest and rejoicing of the Sabbath leading into Sunday worship. We call it "date night with Jesus," since Friday is the night that people in our culture set up dates with that special someone. Since Jesus is our really Special Someone, we have a big group date between our church family of watchmen and Him.

We haven't said as much in this book about fasting as we have in others, but we don't want you to neglect to find a way to combine fasting with your prayer-watching. Begin with a simple fast and go on from there.[1] A seven-day fast can change your destiny. Our habit is to fast as a church body every Monday in addition to calling longer corporate fasts throughout the year at set times or for special needs and national crises.

> *Moreover, when you fast, do not be like the hypocrites, with a sad countenance. For they disfigure their faces that they may appear to men to be fasting. Assuredly, I say to you, they have their reward. But you, when you fast, anoint your head and wash your face, so that you do not appear to men to be fasting, but to your Father who is in the secret place; and your Father who sees in secret will reward you openly* (Matthew 6:16-18).

Notice that it says *when* you fast, not "if" you fast. He trusts we do fast. He trusts we do pray. We can trust He does answer.

There may be times you don't feel the Presence, and that is OK. But ask the Holy Spirit for help. Say, "Holy Spirit, help me." Extol the blood of Christ. "I'm coming, heavenly Father, by the blood of Jesus. Holy Spirit, take me by the hand, and bring me into His presence."

The best person in the world cannot come into His presence except by the blood. No atoning blood, no Presence. So to steward the revival presence, exalt the blood, recognizing your need. The work of the Holy Spirit is to take you and me by the hand and lead us into the presence of God. He makes God real to us as we pray, as we worship, as we give thanks. *"Therefore, brethren, having boldness to enter the Holiest by the blood of Jesus,"* (Heb. 10:19).

When you are watching in His presence, your prayers will be to Him. That may seem like a silly thing to state, but in actuality, most prayers are not to God. What do we mean? Most prayers are not to God because they only raise the concern. If someone says "Cancer," we say, "Oh, cancer—that's really big. That's a hard one." We don't bridge the gap between the cancer and the God who can heal it.

That's why we value *watching* so much. When you watch in prayer, you have time—and the help of others—to get into His presence *first*, before you start reeling off prayer requests. You start thanking Him for who He is before you ever thank Him for what He has just done. You delight in Him as He delights in you.

In His presence, nothing is impossible. But the key is to be more in His presence. We get an audience with the King of kings, whether it's individual or corporate. More and more, as we go on in The Watch, we will need to have more of the sense of the Presence. More and more, we will find ourselves in Isaiah:

> ...*People will say, "Look at what's happened! This is our God! We waited for Him and He showed up and saved us! This God, the one we waited for! Let's celebrate, sing the joys of His salvation. God's hand rests on this mountain!"* (Isaiah 25:9-10 TM).

"Man's chief end is to glorify God, and to enjoy Him forever."[2]

The glory of man is found in relationship with the Glorious Man, and when we stand face-to-face with Him in prayer, a glory greater than that seen on Moses anoints our faces and shines out in the darkness around. This is the hidden power of watching in prayer. Eyes wide open in expectation we see His advent in the earth, basking in His glory as we co-labor with Him in prayer. By it, we are being changed from one glory to another until we stand with that throng that cries, "Hallelujah for the Lord God the Almighty reigns. Let us rejoice and be glad and give Him glory! For the wedding of the Lamb has come, and His bride has made herself ready" (see Rev. 19:6-7).

ENDNOTES

1. See Mahesh Chavda, *The Hidden Power of Prayer and Fasting* (Shippensburg, PA: Destiny Image, 1998).

2. *The Westminster Shorter Catechism* (Question and Answer 1).

For other books, audio tapes,
or other resource material from the authors, contact:

MAHESH CHAVDA MINISTRIES INTERNATIONAL
PO Box 411008
Charlotte, NC 28241
704-541-5300

E-mail: info@watchofthelord.com
Website: www.watchofthelord.com

Additional copies of this book and other
book titles from DESTINY IMAGE are
available at your local bookstore.

Call toll-free: 1-800-722-6774.

Send a request for a catalog to:

Destiny Image® Publishers, Inc.

P.O. Box 310
Shippensburg, PA 17257-0310

*"Speaking to the Purposes of God for this
Generation and for the Generations to Come."*

**For a complete list of our titles,
visit us at www.destinyimage.com.**